CERAMICS

Dolors Ros

DECORATIVE TECHNIQUES

BARRON'S

CERAMICS

Contents

chapter

DECORATING TECHNIQUES

chapter

MAKING PIECES BY HAND

chapter

THE RAW MATERIALS

chapter 4

ENGOBES

chapter 5

GLAZING AND UNDERGLAZING

chapter 6

FIRING

Introduction

Throughout history and in almost every culture, the art of ceramics has been an essential link to cultural identity. The word *ceramics* comes from the Greek, and it refers to clay in all its forms. Thanks to the quality of this material, most museums offer the opportunity to witness how artists have expressed themselves in clay through time. The techniques for working it have not changed through the centuries, from prehistoric times to present day. The Chinese started using the potter's wheel at the beginning of the Neolithic period, Egyptians discovered glaze, and Romans introduced dinnerware and decorating with stamps. Certainly, there is no other craft with so much tradition and with so many possibilities for expression and potential for innovation.

A potter has the privilege of enjoying deep emotions. Only after experiencing the feeling of standing in front of the kiln right after opening its door, can a person understand why potters are so passionate about their work and enjoy it so much. It is simply the constant drive to produce a perfectly finished piece, ready to instill deep feelings in those who contemplate it. The limits between what is considered art and what is not widened considerably during the twentieth century. Nowadays, ceramic pieces make such a powerful artistic statement that they even cross the line into other types of art and media. As the definition of art expands, ceramics acquire increased recognition and strength in the artistic world.

—Dolors Ros

chapter

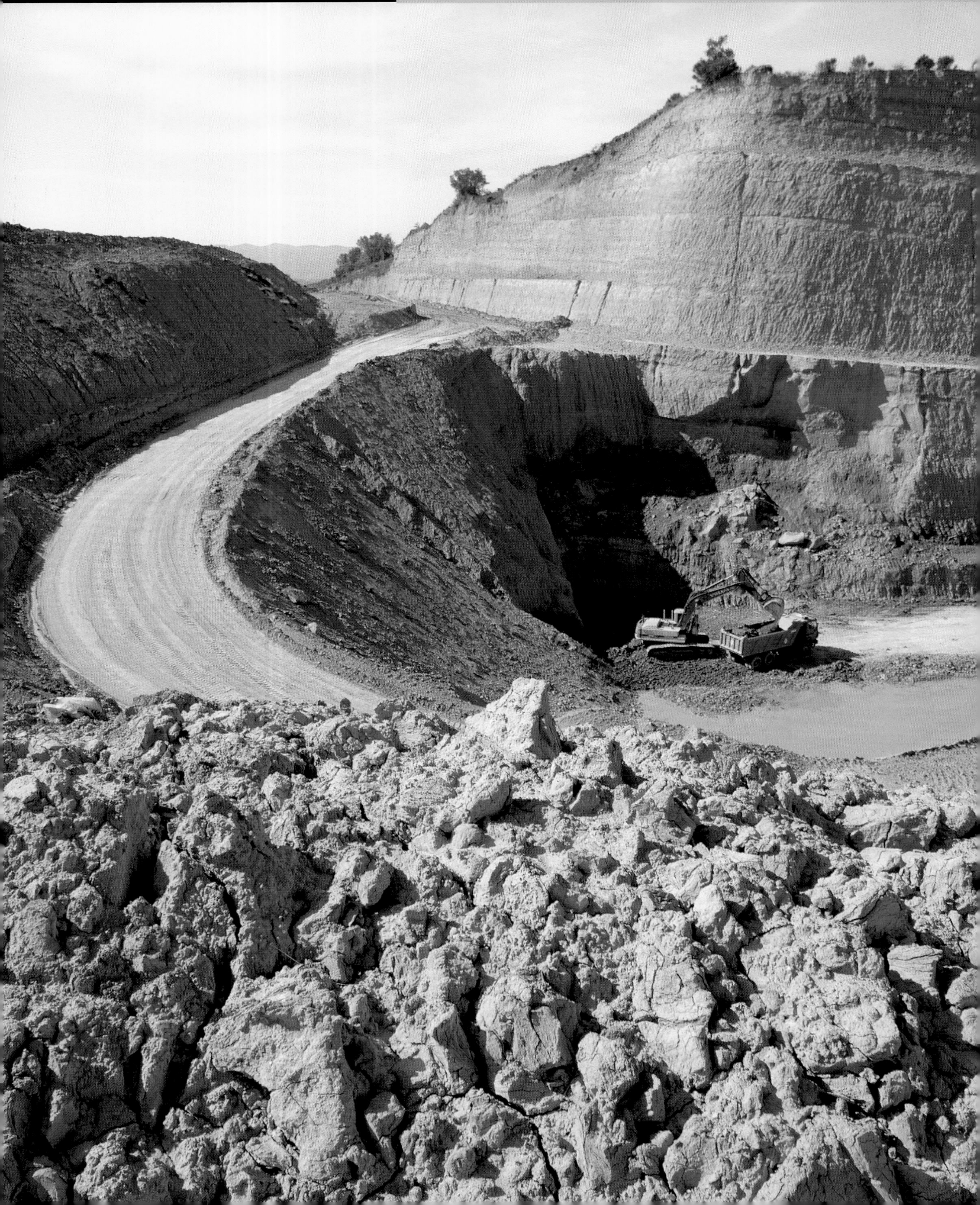

1 The raw materials

Ceramic clay is made from a mixture of different clays and other substances that provide plasticity, porosity, and an approximate firing temperature. Clays must have plasticity to make them easy to shape. They must be sufficiently porous to ensure that they dry evenly. Also, they must have small amounts of melting material so the temperature at which they will melt can be determined. As far as treatments that are applied afterward, such as engobes and glazes, it can be said that engobes add color, bringing the clay piece to life, and glazes make the piece waterproof, thus enabling it to hold liquids.

Clay

Clay is what makes pottery possible. It has a certain plasticity, which allows it to be shaped when mixed with water. Although clay is found everywhere on earth, its properties vary considerably, depending on the area from which the clay comes. Some clays can be used in their extracted form, whereas others must be purified and mixed with water to make them easier to shape.

The origins of clay

Clay is a by-product of the earth's crust—that is, it results from the decomposition of aging rocks exposed to natural elements. Therefore, clay is not found where it is formed but where it settles, in layers of different composition, color, and purity.

The following brief review of the different kinds and most important characteristics of clay explains which kinds are used for which jobs.

Outdoor warehouse with clay waiting to be mixed and treated.

View of recently extracted chunks of clay.

Mechanically processed clay, waiting to be wrapped in plastic for distribution to workshops.

Types of clay

Clay is formed from small crystal compounds, so small that many of them cannot be seen even with the most powerful microscope. They are made up of the mineral kaolin, whose approximate composition is 47 percent silica (SiO_2), 39% alumina (Al_2O_3), and 14 percent water (H_2O).

This chapter focuses on the main characteristics of the types of clay that are most often used: red clay, white clay, porcelain clay, and refractory clay.

Various hand-kneaded clays ready for throwing.

Common red clay

Red clay is normally a brownish gray color, due to its high iron oxide content (Fe_2O_3), which is between 5 and 8 percent. The clay acquires a red or whitish red color when baked, depending on the firing temperature and the atmosphere of the kiln. This clay melts easily, so it should not be heated to more than 2,012°F (1,100°C). The plasticity of the clay makes it perfect for throwing and for making small sculpture pieces.

Common red clay.

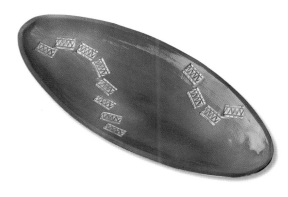

Tray made with red clay decorated with stamps.

White clay

White clay is extracted from small deposits spread all over the world, which is why potters are forced to acquire the clay already prepared. It is normally a light grayish color when it is wet, and an ivory-like or whitish color after it has been baked. The clay is relatively porous and very malleable, and it contains virtually no iron oxide.

Piece made with white clay and later painted.

Although white clay is often used to make pieces in molds, as well as china, wall tile, and bathroom fittings, this clay is also good for throwing.

Its approximate firing temperature ranges between 1,922°F and 2,100°F (1,050°C and 1,150°C). Before glaze is applied, it is a good idea to fire the pieces first at 1,492°F to 1,832°F (800°C to 1,000°C); this first firing is called bisque firing.

White clay.

• Earthenware

The term *earthenware* covers all low-firing white clays. They are generally calciferous and very porous. The color of the natural clay varies from pure white to dark gray. These clays are recommended for use in bisque ware because some glazes do not adhere sufficiently in a single firing.

• Majolica

The name *majolica* describes low-firing white clays covered with a white lead-tin glaze. The Arabs used them in past times.

The name comes from the island of Majorca, Spain, where this type of earthenware originated. From there it was introduced to Italy, where it was prominently used by the Florentine Lucca della Robbia (1400-1481). This clay is also known as faience because it was first used in Faenza, Italy. All majolica have technical characteristics similar to those of white clay.

• Ball clay

Ball clay is generally made of refractory clay, quartz, kaolin, and feldspar. When humid, the clay is a blackish dark gray, but after the first firing it turns ivory pink and becomes strong, waterproof, and refractory. It is a very thin, opaque, and hard clay that resists scratching by metal and partially vitrifies. The recommended firing temperature ranges between 2,012°F and 2,372°F (1,100°C and 1,300°C). The pieces swell partially if exposed to higher temperatures because their components melt.

Ball clay is used for everything, from throwing and shaping to molding.

The main differences between red and earthenware clays are their fusion points and their technical characteristics, because it is considered a high-firing clay.

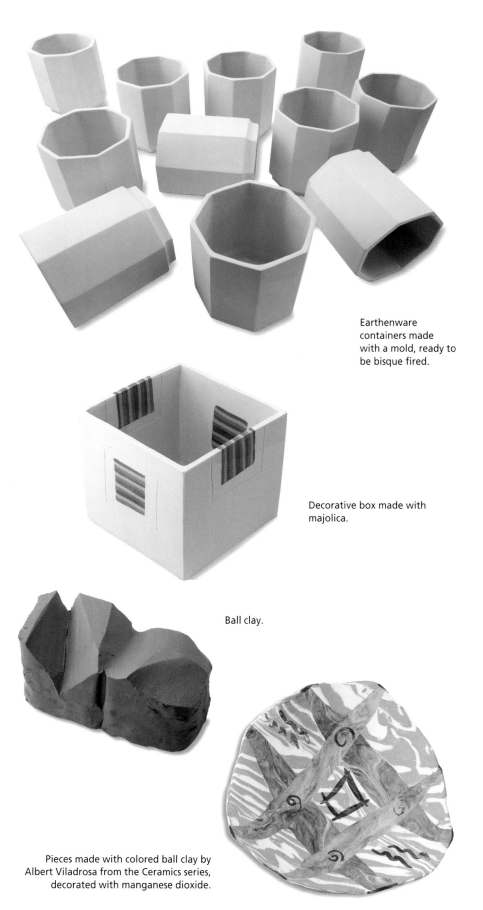

Earthenware containers made with a mold, ready to be bisque fired.

Decorative box made with majolica.

Ball clay.

Pieces made with colored ball clay by Albert Viladrosa from the Ceramics series, decorated with manganese dioxide.

• Porcelain clay

Porcelain clay is made of kaolin, quartz, and feldspar. It is a pure clay that contains no iron oxide. It is light gray when wet, but it turns white upon firing. Its baking temperature ranges between 2,372°F and 2,552°F (1,300°C and 1,400°C). This clay has very little plasticity, so a great deal of expertise is required to work it on the potter's wheel. As a result, the clay is normally used in slip processes. It is highly vitreous and nonporous, and it becomes translucent after baking at high temperatures.

Before glaze firing the piece, it is recommended to do a first firing at 1,492°F to 1,832°F (800°C to 1,000°C) (bisque).

Porcelain clay.

Various pieces of a porcelain china made with a mold and fired at 2,552° F (1,400° C). Design by Porcelanas Pordamsa.

Refractory clay

The refractory clay category includes several types of clays that are hard to define, but they all have one thing in common—their resistance to high temperatures and to contrasts in temperature.

Their plasticity varies greatly, as well as their quartz and alumina content. In general, the most commonly used refractory clays have a high content of grog, or refractory clays that are ground and baked. Their melting point ranges between 2,624°F and 2,912°F (1,440°C and 1,600°C). These clays hardly contract and can be used especially for large pieces and forms.

It is best not to exceed 2,372°F (1,300°C) when working on artistic pieces.

Refractory clay.

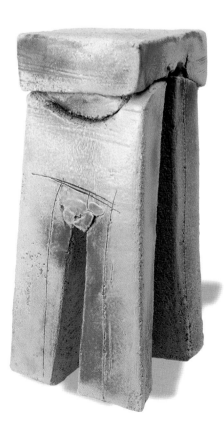

Sculpture made with refractory clay by Madola, from the Doors series.

Colored clays

Colored clays are easily made by adding oxide or dyeing pigment to a type of paste and mixing that evenly with clay. Pigment mixtures can change colors considerably, depending on how they are prepared—that is, whether they use a precise amount of pigment or a random amount.

"Clays for dyeing" refers to common white clays, such as the porcelain clay found in stores.

How to mix pigment colors

Pigments are ceramic materials that provide color, either to the clays or to the glaze. They are classified in two groups: oxides and dyes. Oxides, which are found on the earth's crust, are basic materials that are purified and turned into powder to give color to ceramic pieces. The most commonly used oxides are copper oxide, which in oxidizing conditions is green; oxide cobalt, which provides blue tones; iron oxide, which produces yellow tones when mixed with a glaze, and earthy brown tones when mixed with clay or engobe; chromium oxide, which produces an opaque olive green color; manganese dioxide, which provides brown and purple tones; and tin oxide, which produces grayish green tones. All these oxides can be mixed with clay in a proportion of 0.5 to 6 percent. If these amounts are exceeded, care must be taken so that the firing temperature does not exceed 1,868°F (1,020°C), because the oxide could act as a melting agent and reduce the fusion point of the clay, which would produce defects during the firing.

The second group of pigments is the dyes, which are basic industrial materials or ready-to-use products prepared by mechanical processes that include the remaining range of colors.

They are mixed with the clay in a proportion of 5 to 20 percent, depending on whether a lighter or darker color is desired. They can be purchased at any specialized store and they can be called colorants or pigments for dyeing clay or engobes.

Much care should be taken when mixing the pigment. One of two methods can be used; however, each yields very different results. The most logical and precise method involves using a specific, measured amount of pigment. The other method involves mixing a random amount directly into the paste, gradually until the desired color is achieved. This method should be used only if the color that results is not a matter of concern or if the same tone does not need to be replicated.

Pigments.

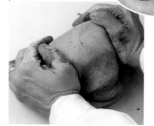

1- Prepare a paste of white earthenware, which can be purchased at any ceramics store already moist. Weigh the desired amount—for example, 3½ oz (100 gm).

2- Weigh the minimum and maximum amounts as explained in the previous page—that is between 5 and 20 percent pigment, according to the color intensity desired.

3- Mix the pigment with the clay by shaping it into a bowl, to make sure that no pigment is wasted.

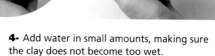

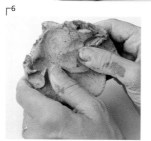

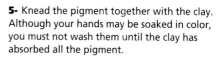

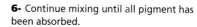

4- Add water in small amounts, making sure the clay does not become too wet.

5- Knead the pigment together with the clay. Although your hands may be soaked in color, you must not wash them until the clay has absorbed all the pigment.

6- Continue mixing until all pigment has been absorbed.

7- When the color of the clay is completely even, the clay can be kneaded on a porous surface until a homogeneous paste has been formed.

8- Cut the paste from time to time to make sure the color is even.

9- When the clay and the pigment are completely mixed, wrap the clay with transparent plastic so the color is clearly visible and the clay does not dry out. Then, label the package with the name of the pigment and the proportion.

10- Before you engage in any project, it is a good idea to make a small sample so you will know the amount of pigment needed to achieve the desired color and even the appropriate glaze.

11- Bake the sample and save it for future projects.

Care when handling clay

Avoiding errors from the very beginning is as important as knowing how to give a piece shape and color. Knowing what the optimum moisture point is, how to bond the walls, or how to avoid air bubbles that produce cracks and breaks during drying, and explosions during firing, is so important that it is necessary to take precautions before moving along with any project. Good wedging must follow, and if possible, machine wedging is best.

Wedging

Clays are wedged to eliminate air bubbles and to make them soft, malleable, and consistent all the way through. During the wedging process, the clay is kneaded by hand to make it malleable.

If the clay is soft and sticky, then it has too much moisture. It must be kneaded on a plaster bat or be allowed to rest on this same base for a while before it is reworked. If, on the other hand, the clay cracks as it is being worked, then it is too dry. Several pieces must be cut with a thread and wet with a sponge. Then, they must be mixed together and kneaded on a flat surface—although not over plaster—until the clay becomes soft and malleable again.

These recovery methods are applied only if the clay is too wet or too dry.

Machine kneading of the clay, called vacuum kneading (the tool is a cookie press).

1- Clay that is too wet must be left to dry on top of a plaster base or on any other porous surface before it is kneaded.

2- To knead clay by hand, apply light pressure on the entire mass, pressing it from the outside in.

3- Next, apply pressure slowly, giving the clay an elongated shape and removing all the air bubbles.

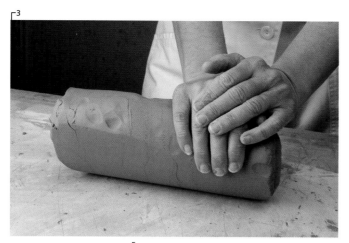

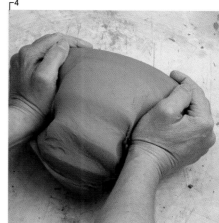

4- Continue to push the clay slowly toward its center, always going on to pressing the center of the ball.

5- At the same time as the mass is turned toward the center, try to raise it and twist it slowly with light pats.

6- Then, press and push with a circular stroke, to force the flat particles of clay into a parallel configuration, so the clay will be more malleable and even.

Air bubbles

Any air bubbles trapped inside the thick walls of a piece can pose considerable danger during firing. Why? The air turns into steam, which increases in pressure against the walls that impede its expansion. If the air pressure is high, the piece can explode and break, damaging other pieces close by, and even the kiln. To avoid air bubbles in the clay, the only solution is to wedge it thoroughly, either by machine or by hand.

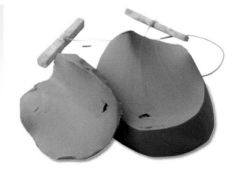

These are the different bubble sizes that can form during wedging. They must be avoided at all cost.

Air bubbles or excessive moisture on the walls or at the base of the pieces can result in breakage inside the kiln during the first levels of firing (around 482°F to 662°F [250°C to 350°C]).

Shrinkage

The water that allows the clay to be worked is called plasticity water, and that constitutes between 30 and 35 percent of the weight of the wet clay. When the water evaporates, the clay's particles contract. The smaller the particles, the greater the contraction—and, therefore, the greater the risk of getting cracks or defects. A clay with large particles, such as refractory clay, shrinks much less. A ceramic piece does its shrinking during drying, when all the water that provides flexibility to the piece evaporates, giving it the rigidity of leather, and during firing, when the hydrogen and the oxygen that are contained within as chemical water must find a way to leave. It is during firing that the clay shrinks permanently, between 8 and 20 percent, depending on its quality.

Clay drying in the sun.

Drying

The drying of an unfired piece, unless it has some parts that are thicker than others, is slow and regular, with no problems other than shrinking, as long as the drying takes place at room temperature.

Improper drying—that is, with too much heat or in a draft—produces irregular shrinkage, which can cause some parts to have defects or to break. Normally, clay walls should be no more than ⅜ inch (1 cm) thick.

If the clay object is too thick or its walls have too many variations, a wet cloth or a piece of plastic must be placed over the object, to promote even drying, and the cloth or plastic should be dampened from time to time. It is a good idea to uncover the pieces for short periods of time, to encourage the drying. The handles, hollow areas, protruding parts, lids, arms and legs of figures, and complementary pieces must be wrapped with small pieces of plastic or with wet cloths so they do not dry too fast. The rims of bowls must also be wrapped for the duration of the drying process, to ensure that they dry evenly. When the clay is left to dry, it becomes resistant and hard, and even though it still contains some moisture, it has already lost its plasticity.

Bowl built from shapes that are left exposed as decoration.

1- Before covering a piece that appears to be too hard, it is advisable to dampen it with a spray.

2- Then it must be covered with a piece of plastic that has also been dampened.

3- Pieces that must be dried very slowly should be covered and uncovered for a few hours at a time each day.

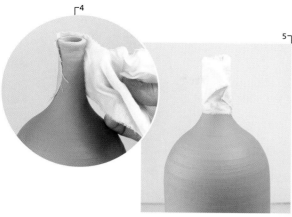

4 and 5- The pieces begin to dry in the areas where the walls are thinnest, which is generally around the rim. In this case, a wet cloth can be placed on the top part to soften the clay walls.

6- When the wet cloth is in place over the driest area, the entire piece is covered with plastic to encourage slow, even drying.

7- When pieces dry too fast, and their walls do not have the same thickness all the way through, the base may crack. This is an example of a piece that has dried too fast.

8- Clay pieces can crack at any time during drying if the process is incorrect. Even after being buffed, cracks can appear on the walls, which is why they must dry very slowly.

Recycling the clay

Recycling leftover clay from a potter's wheel is a subject very seldom mentioned, even though it can save money. When clay is left unattended on a table for some time and it dries too much, it cannot be used for working on the wheel. The same thing happens with pieces that break while practicing.

Clay that has hardened must be placed in the sun or by a heater so it finishes drying completely. After that, water is added until the clay dissolves, and then the resulting liquid clay is spread on a concave plaster board until it reaches the ideal texture to be wedged and worked on the wheel again.

1- Clay that has become unusable because it has hardened is placed in the sun or near a heater so it loses all its moisture and dries out completely.

2- When the clay dries, water is added until the clay completely dissolves, at which time it is mixed with a mixer until it acquires the consistency of a thick puree.

3- When the clay turns into a thick puree, it is poured over a concave plaster board or any porous container, until it acquires the ideal consistency for wedging and for reworking on the wheel.

Tools

Many types of tools are available for working pottery, but only after experimenting with them for a while can a potter know which ones are going to be used all the time. In general, most potters make their own tools or acquire them over time from shops that specialize in tools or plastics or other such trades. Many of the best tools are fashioned from common utensils, which after sanding or sharpening become excellent cutting tools.

Commonly used materials

• Rolling pins, canvas, and wood strips

In the kitchen, the rolling pin is commonly used for working the dough for pizzas and pies. In pottery, it is used for rolling sheets of clay. To maintain the rolling pin, it must be rubbed gently after each use to dislodge any leftover clay and then wiped clean with a wet sponge. Rolling pins are available in different sizes.

Canvas can be found in any fabric store. It is used as base when making slabs, and it promotes shrinking of the clay when it begins to lose moisture.

The wood that is placed under the canvas serves as support and makes it easier to handle the slab made with the rolling pin or with the mill.

The strips of wood control the thickness of the piece being made, therefore it is important to have an assortment of sizes.

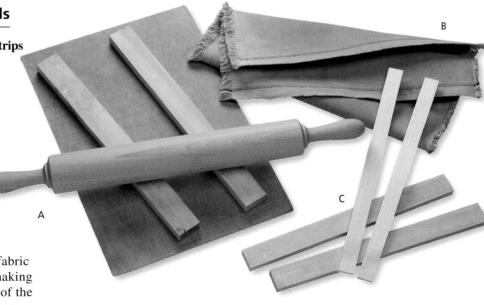

Rolling pin (A), canvas (B), and wood strips (C).

• Sponges

The synthetic sponges that are used with pottery are useful for giving the first finishing touches to the pieces. They are also good for creating decorative effects.

Sponges

Slip trailers.

Mortar.

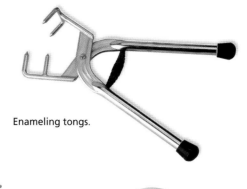

Enameling tongs.

Pot and brush.

Bowls.

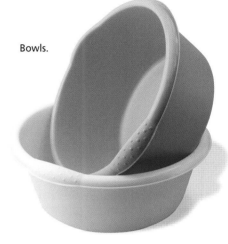

Sieves and funnel.

Mixer.   Sprayer.

• Slip trailers

Slip trailers are used for making decorations, to add water to the paste or glaze, or to absorb the excess water from a solution left unattended. They must be washed after each use to prevent contamination and any change in color.

• Mortar

Nowadays, almost all commercial ceramic products come in powder form, which makes dilution and mixture easier. However, some are sold in granules, and a mortar must be used to crush and grind them.

• Enameling tongs

Enameling tongs make it possible to hold any small piece being enameled with the least contact, thus avoiding fingerprints on the pieces.

• Pot and brush

When working at the wheel, the hands must be dampened with water, which can be stored in a pot placed nearby. The excess liquid clay that comes off the wheel can also be deposited in it. The brush is useful for adding liquid clay to the piece.

• Bowls

Bowls and washbasins are practical for mixing or recovering liquid that has been used in the pouring method.

• Sieves and funnels

Sieves are used to filter ceramic materials that are used for decorating. They come in different screen sizes, which is indicated with a number. And, they help eliminate impurities from the mixture and, with those impurities, possible defects that could occur when glazing. Funnels are used for pouring glazes or engobes into storage containers that have narrow mouths.

• Mixer

The mixer makes mixing the clay much easier. When working with large quantities of clay, it is important to mix the clay properly, and this tool is very useful for making the mixtures consistent all the way through.

• Sprayer

A sprayer is used to spray water on pieces that are beginning to dry so the process can be slow, and therefore safe. A sprayer is used countless times during the work process.

• **Scale**

There are two types of scales: the manual ones, which use weights, and the electronic, or digital ones. The first type guarantees accurate measurement, whereas the second type, especially if it is not precise, risks slight variations in the measurements. It is best to use a manual scale to weigh oxides and dyes that require precise measurements.

• **Turntable**

Thanks to the turntable, a piece can be worked on more comfortably because there is no need for changing the position of the object by lifting it. This also prevents possible defects. It can also be used as a base for decorating. Some turntables, like the one in the picture, are equipped with an accessory that is used as support for painting lines on circular pieces.

• **Face mask**

Face masks are necessary for safety and hygiene, especially when handling products that give off dust or when using a compressor for glazing.

• **Spoons and labels**

Spoons are used for stirring small amounts of solution and for handling products with more precision. They are also used for a decorative technique called burnishing. The labels are used for marking the content of any product.

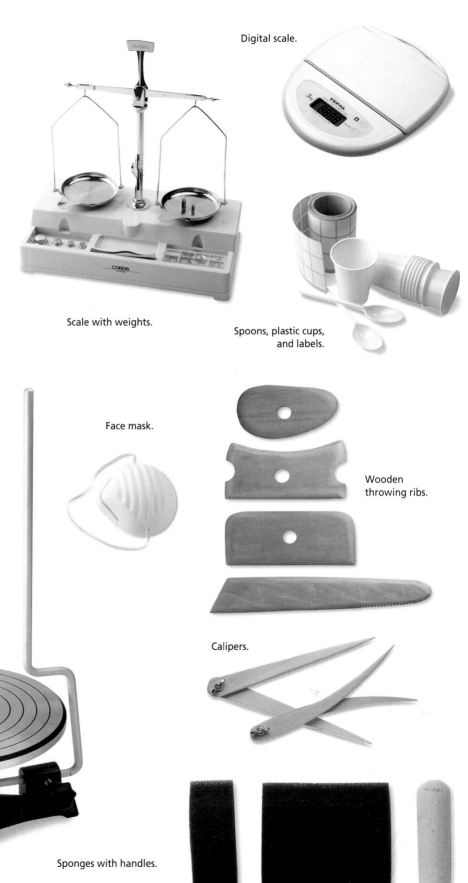

Digital scale.

Scale with weights.

Spoons, plastic cups, and labels.

Face mask.

Wooden throwing ribs.

Calipers.

Turntable with a vertical bar for decorating.

Sponges with handles.

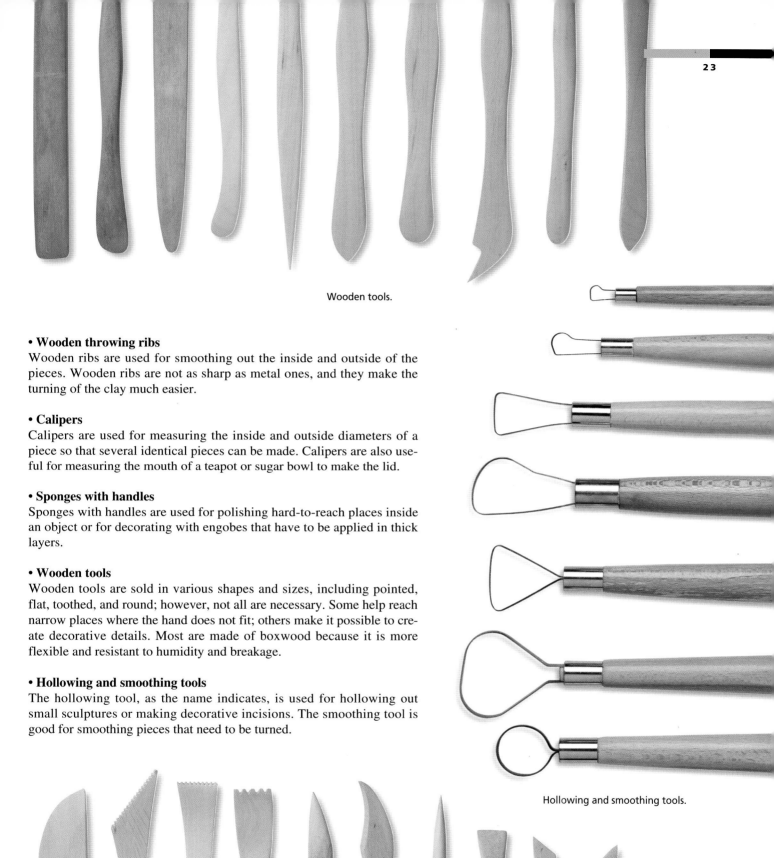

Wooden tools.

Hollowing and smoothing tools.

Wooden tools.

• Wooden throwing ribs
Wooden ribs are used for smoothing out the inside and outside of the pieces. Wooden ribs are not as sharp as metal ones, and they make the turning of the clay much easier.

• Calipers
Calipers are used for measuring the inside and outside diameters of a piece so that several identical pieces can be made. Calipers are also useful for measuring the mouth of a teapot or sugar bowl to make the lid.

• Sponges with handles
Sponges with handles are used for polishing hard-to-reach places inside an object or for decorating with engobes that have to be applied in thick layers.

• Wooden tools
Wooden tools are sold in various shapes and sizes, including pointed, flat, toothed, and round; however, not all are necessary. Some help reach narrow places where the hand does not fit; others make it possible to create decorative details. Most are made of boxwood because it is more flexible and resistant to humidity and breakage.

• Hollowing and smoothing tools
The hollowing tool, as the name indicates, is used for hollowing out small sculptures or making decorative incisions. The smoothing tool is good for smoothing pieces that need to be turned.

• Scissors, cutters, and pencils

Scissors, cutters, and pencils are all useful tools. They are used for cutting out stencils and resists for decorating as well as for other tasks.

• Potter's knives and serrated scraper

Knives are used for all types of decorative tasks, including scraping and engraving. The serrated scraper can be a piece of an old hacksaw blade sharpened by the user according to need. We consider this an essential tool.

• Big and small brushes

Various brushes are used for working with pottery, each for a specific task. Throughout this book, their main functions and characteristics are shown and explained. Small flat brushes are used for making wide lines and for specific decorative effects that make the background of the piece transparent. Round ones are used for more detailed decoration and for spattering, whereas larger flat brushes are ideal for decorating large surfaces or for removing dust from the sgraffito. Brushes should be maintained in perfect working condition. Cleaning and preserving the hair is essential, even if it is synthetic. They should be stored flat or upright, with the bristles facing up in the latter case.

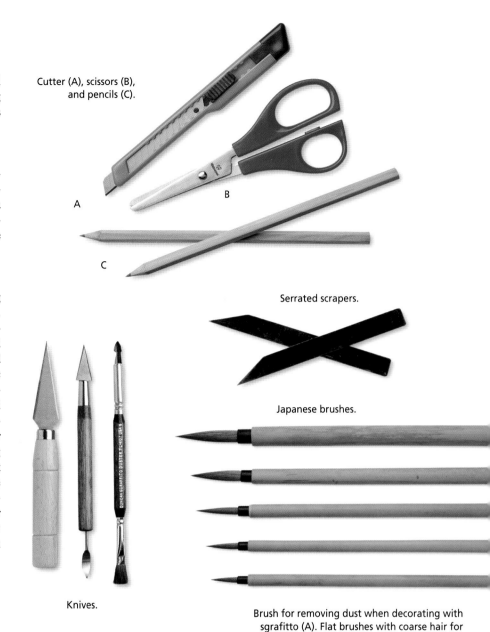

Cutter (A), scissors (B), and pencils (C).

Serrated scrapers.

Japanese brushes.

Knives.

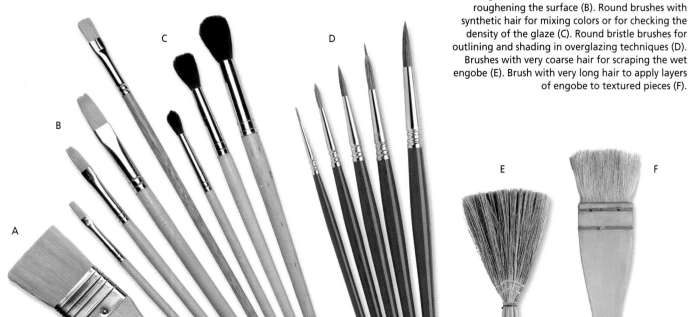

Brush for removing dust when decorating with sgrafitto (A). Flat brushes with coarse hair for roughening the surface (B). Round brushes with synthetic hair for mixing colors or for checking the density of the glaze (C). Round bristle brushes for outlining and shading in overglazing techniques (D). Brushes with very coarse hair for scraping the wet engobe (E). Brush with very long hair to apply layers of engobe to textured pieces (F).

• **Potter's needles and hole cutters**
The potter's needles, with their sharp and long points, are useful for outlining a design to be engraved later or simply for decorating.

Hole cutters, which are also used for a wide variety of decorating tasks, come in various sizes. They are used for piercing because they have sharp and angled points that allow greater precision and less possibility of breakage.

• **Cutting wire**
Cutting wire is used for cutting clay directly from a purchased block. It has a pair of wooden dowels at the ends that can be grasped and pulled with force, without danger of cutting oneself. This wire is often used at the wheel to cut pieces made on the turntable.

• **Metal tools**
Metal tools come in many shapes and are commonly used for doing the final touches and for removing the wet clay from the pieces before they are taken off the wheel. They are also used to smoothe, bond, and polish in different techniques.

• **Wheel and sharpener**
The wheel is used for making incisions on hard clays. The sharpener, besides its normal use, can be used for decorating on soft clays or making stamps and cutting incisions.

• **Sandpaper and steel wool**
Sandpaper is used for touching up pieces after firing, especially decorations made with colored clay, to ensure that the pieces are completely clean. A pad of fine steel wool is useful for finishing the piece before the first firing (bisque), to make it completely smooth.

• **Comb and thread**
A comb is used for texturing the clay when it is still wet. The thread is useful for cutting the sides of the pieces being worked on the wheel, to make square, triangular, or hexagonal cuts.

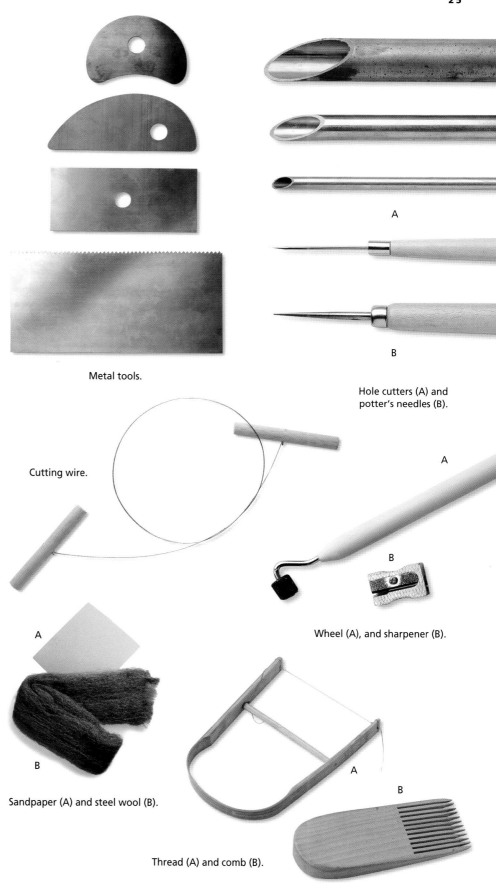

Metal tools.

Hole cutters (A) and potter's needles (B).

Cutting wire.

Wheel (A), and sharpener (B).

Sandpaper (A) and steel wool (B).

Thread (A) and comb (B).

Making pieces by hand

Making ceramic pieces by hand can be summarized into three basic techniques, which have been used since the beginnings of clay production: modeling, throwing, and molding. Many variations and personal designs are derived from those three. Knowing which is the most appropriate method for each technique requires professional expertise, and depends on the number of pieces that you wish to make.

To produce pieces that have artistic value or certain complexity of form, it is best to create them by hand; however, if the project requires making a service for coffee or a set of china pieces, the method of choice should be the potter's wheel or a mold.

Modeling techniques

In ceramics, there are a handful of basic techniques for modeling, and most potters use the same ones over and over, relying on professional experience and personal formulas to combine them and to create special effects. This book not only explains the processes but also illustrates some of the decorative ideas mentioned in the previous chapter, which when combined can produce impressive results.

The different modeling techniques

Many modeling techniques have been developed through the ages, but the basic principles have not changed that much. The most common modeling techniques are pinching, coiling, slab building, forming with molds, and modeling on the potter's wheel. Any other method can be used along with these techniques, or can be combined with them. Perhaps the most difficult part is knowing which method to use for a particular result.

The most well known method—and the one that works well with a wide variety of pieces—is the coiling technique. It is the oldest method known for making china and containers for liquids, but it is also appropriate for making utensils.

The pinching method is more useful for creating small objects, such as coffee or teacups. The objects may end up looking more rustic and irregular, but they will surely bear the trademark of a piece that was made completely by hand.

When a project calls for many pieces to be made in a short time, the most appropriate method, without a doubt, is modeling on the potter's wheel, although combinations can be created using the turned piece as a base. The advantage of starting with a turned piece is that the object will have good volume and consistency. Furthermore it can be easily achieved with little intervention, yet with excellent artistic results.

Figures made with slabs of refractory clay, and decorated with oxides by Teresa Gironés, from the Figures series.

Bowl formed on the potter's wheel from red clay.

Decorative vase made with colored coils of earthenware clay.

These pieces were made with coils. Originally intended for storing liquids (water, wine, or oil), these pieces are now an attractive decorative complement for the garden.

Pinching

Pinching consists of working the clay by pinching it with the fingers. It is a useful method for making small pieces—and ideal for beginners because it is easy and fun. The clay must be perfectly kneaded, and it should have enough moisture so that it can be modeled.

There are many ways for making decorative objects using the pinching technique. The objects can be round or triangular, they can be decorated by patting them lightly with a piece of wood, and they can have handles, feet, borders, and other additions. In other words, they can be made as simple or as complex as desired.

1- To begin, make a ball the size of a small orange with a piece of wet clay.

2- Cradle the ball of clay in one hand to protect it, while working it with the thumb of the other hand toward the center.

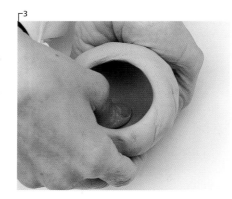

3- Turn the base holding it between the thumb and index fingers, pressing while turning.

4- Continue pressing the same way while moving up to the rim.

5- The hand's heat may cause the clay to dry, and cracks may appear. To avoid this, periodically smooth out the surface with a wet finger.

6- Once the piece is finished, turn it over to smooth out the walls and the base to add the foot.

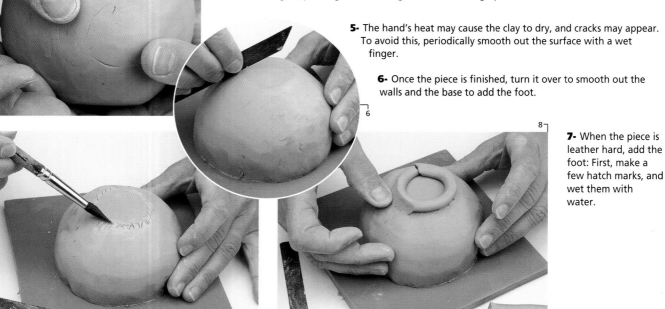

7- When the piece is leather hard, add the foot: First, make a few hatch marks, and wet them with water.

8- To make the foot form a coil, incorporate it using your fingers.

9 and 10- Smooth the inside of the coil with a wooden tool, and then go over it again with a finger.

11- After the piece is finished but before leaving it to dry, go over it with a wet sponge.

12- Cut the rim flat with a sharp knife.

13- Wet the rim with a sponge.

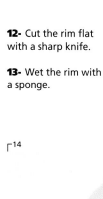

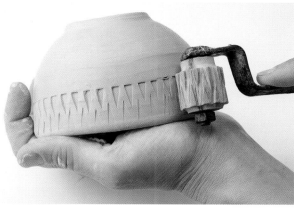

14- If you wish to apply decorative designs, you must do it before the piece dries out completely.

15- The rim has potential for cracking as soon as it begins to dry. To avoid this, place the piece face down over a wet cloth for a few minutes until it recovers the lost moisture.

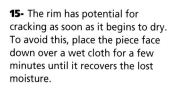

16- The finished piece before firing.

Coiling

Coiling is one of the oldest techniques in existence: It dates back to 6000 B.C. To follow the use, expansion, and development of this technique through time and different civilizations, one needs only to observe the evolution of mankind, throughout which ancestors solved their problems and needs by combining practical designs with artistic forms.

To practice this technique, certain precision of movement is required, as well as some skill and time to enjoy it. Various shapes can be made using the coiling technique, including cylindrical forms, openmouthed or closemouthed round shapes, and even pieces where the coils are stacked over flat surfaces and left exposed.

The first step involves checking the clay to make sure that it is flexible enough and that it contains enough moisture to make the coils without them cracking or sticking to the work surface. To keep the pieces moist during the process, they must be kept covered with plastic until they are completely finished.

The drying process of objects made with coils, either big or small, must be slow to ensure that they dry evenly.

How to make cylindrical shapes

The best way to start using the coiling technique is to attempt a cylindrical piece. This will be an educational process, not only on how to arrange the coils correctly but also on how to get used to following certain work habits, because cylindrical shapes are easy to correct. A flat implement is all that is needed.

1- Make a slab either with coils or by machine. Then place it on a turntable. Mark and cut the circular shape, which will be the base of the piece.

2- Remove the excess clay from the base.

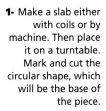

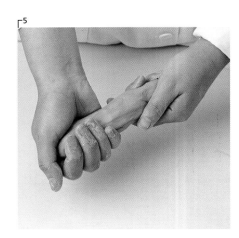

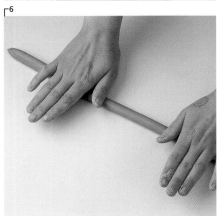

3- Make a few hatch marks on the base.

4- Wet the base with some slip to adhere the first coil.

5- Begin by making the first coil from a piece that you previously rolled out by hand.

6- Then, roll the clay coil on a flat surface with the palm of your hand, making sure not to apply much pressure so the coil keeps its round shape and does not flatten.

7- If the clay cracks while being rolled, dampen it with a little bit of water, or knead it again until the clay regains flexibility and moisture.

8- Place the coil over the surface moistened with slip. Press the clay with your fingers, down first and then upward.

9- When you work coils with your fingers, there is normally a point when you can no longer press them to the base enough without them losing their shape. When this happens, it is a good idea to use a wooden tool for the task.

10- If the clay is not soft enough before another coil is placed, score a few lines, and apply liquid clay.

11- As you arrange one coil on top of the other, the rim will be uneven. Every five or six coils you will have to even out the rim, cutting a little into it to make it completely straight. Then, make a few hatch marks, wet it with liquid clay, and add the next coil. The exterior walls should also be smoothed out with a throwing rib.

12- While evening out the rim, you can fill in the gaps with any excess clay that has come off the piece, using the throwing rib.

13- The coils can be used to create different shapes. If you choose cylindrical ones, you only need to place one coil on top of the other, making sure none stand out, and even them out with a straight tool.

14- Finally, smooth the rim with a wet sponge, and let the piece dry.

How to make round shapes

Whether you decide to make an open-mouthed or closemouthed bowl, or a round shape, the placement of the coils changes according to the chosen cylindrical form. The base, on the other hand, is formed the same as that of the base for the cylindrical shape explained before.

It is always a good idea to make a drawing of the object that you wish to make on a piece of paper before you start with the clay. Also, making a life-size model with sturdy cardboard or with very thin wood can help you achieve greater precision in your project: While you are making your piece, you can compare it with the model to ensure that you are following the correct shape.

1- To make a concave or openmouthed piece, arrange the coils outward, making sure that they do not protrude too much. If the shape is too open, you will need to complete the process in two or three sessions, to prevent the piece from falling apart. It is very important to join the coils well from the inside, because it is in this part that the piece is wider and the outside is weaker.

2- For the second half of the piece, arrange the coils inward as you advance toward the top so the neck begins to narrow gradually.

3- On the other hand, for closemouth pieces, you must join the coils from the outside, as you get close to the top, because it is difficult to join them correctly from the inside. The joint between the coils must be tight and smooth.

Decorative elements can be introduced with the coiling method—for example, using colored coils or finishing the neck with a different color clay—while the piece is being worked on. Smooth out the neck on the curved side using a throwing rib to shape.

1- The entire piece can be made from a single color, or you can experiment with different colors. In this case, a straight mouth is being formed with a different color. Once the piece is halfway finished, before you put the first colored coil in place, wet the border with liquid clay.

2- Place the first colored coil.

3- Continue arranging the coils, following the procedure explained for the cylinder, by joining them from the inside and smoothing the walls with a wooden tool.

4- Another coiling method that can save you time is to arrange three or four coils one after the other to ensure they are straight.

5- Then join them together using your fingers or a wooden tool.

6- The finished piece before firing.

Pieces with exposed coils over flat surfaces

To make a piece where the coils are attached to a flat surface and left exposed, begin by using a plaster mold, on which a slab is made from a colored clay of your choice and then cut to size.

1- Arrange spiral coils around the edges.

2- Fill the gaps with slip.

3- Smooth it out with your fingers until it is completely flat.

4- Cut off the excess clay.

5- View of the inside of the finished piece.

Slab building

The technique of forming a piece from clay that has been cut into slabs is referred to as slab building. Before making the slabs, the clay must be kneaded and compressed until a mass that is consistent all the way through is formed. To make the slabs, you will need a wood surface, a piece of cloth or canvas, two wooden sticks the thickness of the slab that you want to make to serve as rolling guides, and a kitchen rolling pin. You must decide on the size of the slab beforehand, because if the roller is too short, the slab may end up being too narrow.

The finished slabs should be handled carefully and only as much as necessary so they do not warp or crack later. It is a good idea to use a sheet of newspaper or a piece of cloth as a base to help prevent the clay from shrinking while it dries.

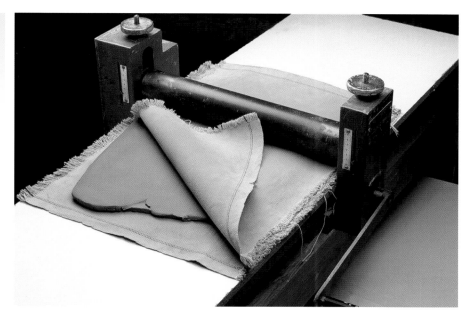

Another method for making slabs is with a roller. This machine will make the job easier, and it will form any size slab, no matter how small.

1- Before you make the slabs, decide which design you want and make a model to determine the exact dimensions of the piece.

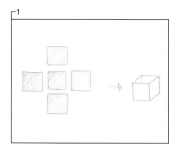
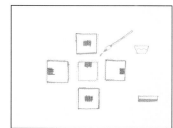
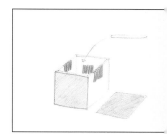

2- Take a lump of clay in the desired color. Arrange several wooden sticks, each 1/8 inch (3 mm) thick, in two groups of the same height. Arrange one set on the left of the lump of clay and one on the right.

3- Cut the slabs by pressing hard against the wood guides with the wire. Take a different colored clay, and continue cutting slabs.

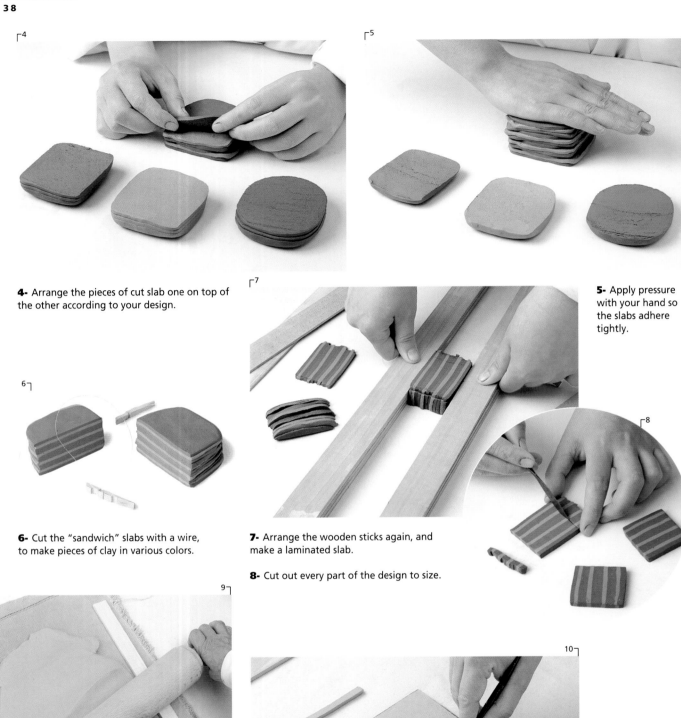

4- Arrange the pieces of cut slab one on top of the other according to your design.

5- Apply pressure with your hand so the slabs adhere tightly.

6- Cut the "sandwich" slabs with a wire, to make pieces of clay in various colors.

7- Arrange the wooden sticks again, and make a laminated slab.

8- Cut out every part of the design to size.

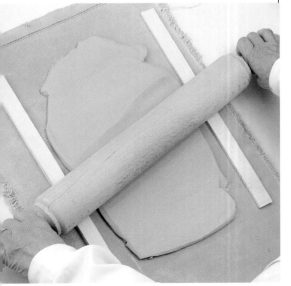

9- Prepare a slab of white clay with the rolling pin.

10- Cut the slab to size according to the design.

11- Cut out the white slab, and brush it with slip to incorporate the laminated piece.

12- Attach the colored piece to the white slab, brushing them with slip to make sure they are joined together perfectly.

13- Press the slab on its sides with a couple of wooden sticks, to make sure they are straight.

14- Roll over the entire piece with the rolling pin to flatten.

15- When the four walls and the base are finished, arrange each piece in its correct location, before cutting them at a 45-degree angle and attaching them together.

16- Cut three sides of each slab at a 45-degree angle, except for the base, whose four sides will be cut.

17- Make several hatch marks.

18- Brush slip on as if it were glue.

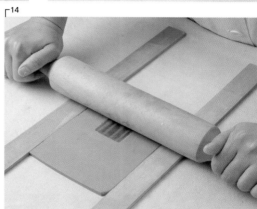

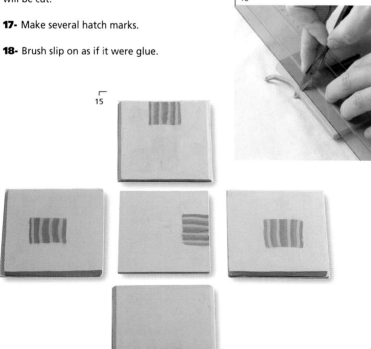

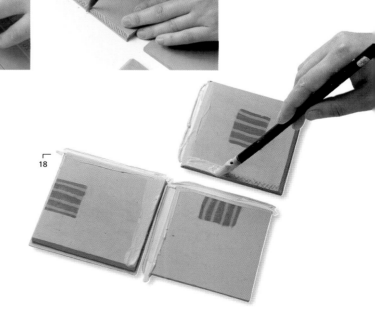

19- Put all pieces together. The joints formed by the slabs of clay must fit tightly together so they do not warp or crack. To reinforce the corners, add small, thin clay coils from the inside.

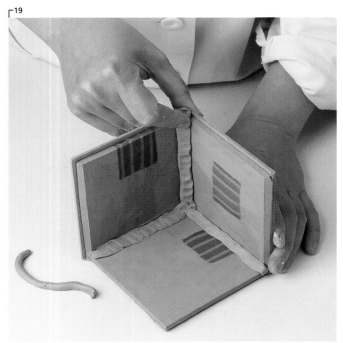

20- Place a small coil on the outside of the joint.

21- Clean the walls with a metal rib.

22- When the object is finished, place a piece of newspaper inside of it to prevent the walls from warping, and wrap it in plastic for a couple of days.

23- Unwrap the piece from time to time so it dries slowly, and continue working on the decoration.

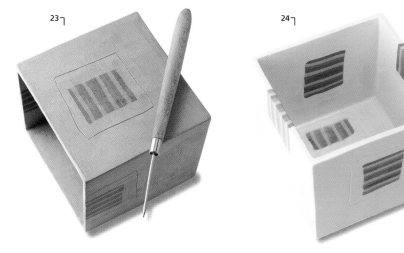

24- The finished piece, still drying.

Slab built piece with inlays

The inlay pieces formed with a rolling pin or by machine can be made either with soft or hard clay. In either case, the clays must have similar consistency and body, otherwise cracks may appear.

1 and 2- First, prepare the clay that you want to use for the project. The example here uses a *neriage* paste, which is a mixture of two different-colored clays. Note that the clays are not mixed completely, so a water effect is achieved.

3- Prepare several very fine coils.

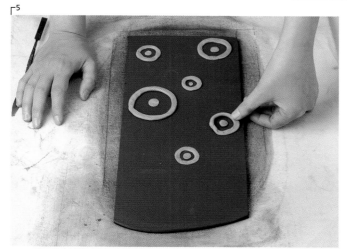

4- Form circles of different sizes with the coils.

5- Place these circles on a different-colored sheet of clay that has already been finished.

6- Place two wooden sticks, 1/8 inch (3 mm) thick, one at each side of the sheet with the inlay pieces. Then, roll the pin as many times as needed until it is completely smooth and the same thickness of the sticks. No bulging or cracking should be present.

7- Cut the piece to the size required by the model.

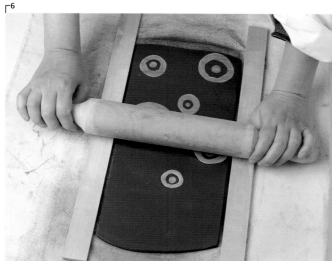

8- Place a sheet of paper over the slab, and roll it around a bottle. This will help you get the form that you want.

9- Cut off the excess clay, make hatch marks, and brush it with slip.

10- Join the edges with a light pressure so the piece does not lose its shape.

11- Stand the bottle up to make the base.

12- Cut the base to match the piece.

13- Make the usual hatch marks, and apply the slip.

14- Attach the base to the piece.

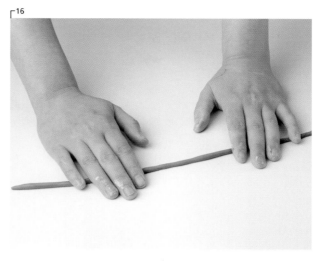

15- Remove the bottle and the paper by pulling up slowly. The piece is now formed.

16 and 17- Place a coil on the inside, along the joint, and attach it by applying light pressure.

18- Smooth out the surface of the cylinder with a metal rib to remove the leftover pieces of clay.

19- Smooth out the decorative areas with a metal rib to give them definition.

20- After you have fired the piece, sand it with a fine-grit sandpaper to smooth it and to give it the final finish.

21- View of the finished, sanded piece.

22- Piece finished and fired.

Modeling with forms

Some pieces are made using ready-made forms, by placing the clay inside of them or over something that supports them and shapes them at the same time. The best materials for this purpose are those that absorb moisture and allow the clay to dry easily—for example plaster of paris. When the object is shaped on a form that does not absorb the clay's excess water, a piece of newspaper or cloth must be placed between them. The cloth can be wrinkled so its design will create a decorative effect. Refractory clays will hardly form any cracks when they are drying because these clays contract much less.

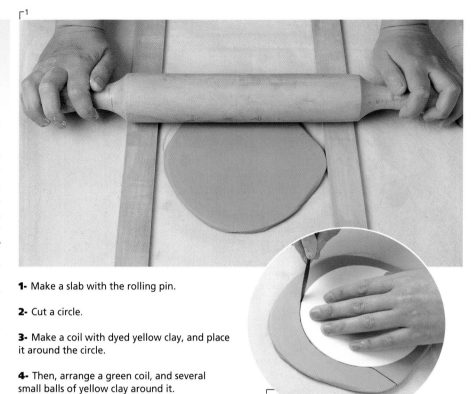

1- Make a slab with the rolling pin.

2- Cut a circle.

3- Make a coil with dyed yellow clay, and place it around the circle.

4- Then, arrange a green coil, and several small balls of yellow clay around it.

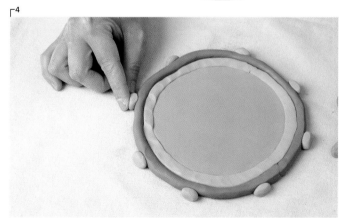

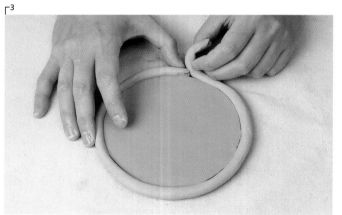

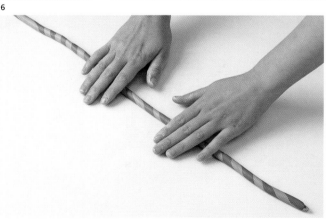

5- Form one coil with white clay and a second one with green clay, and braid the two coils together.

6- Roll them to completely combine them.

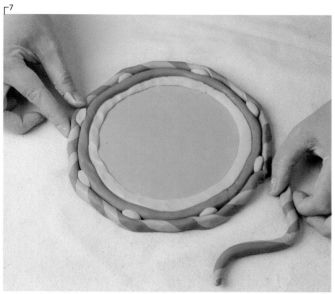

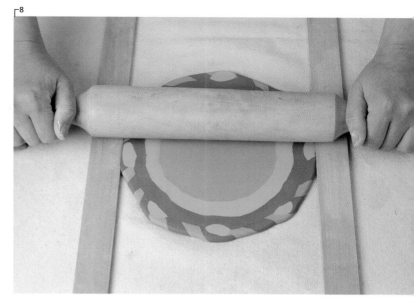

7- Add the braided coil around the circle.

8- Roll over the entire piece again with the rolling pin to ensure that it is joined completely and that it is has the same thickness all over.

9- Place the slab on a convex mold, made in the studio with plaster of paris, gypsum, or any other readily available plastic object.

10- To help form the slab of clay to the mold, tap it gently using a wooden stick with a nylon stocking carefully folded and glued to it. The stocking is used because it has little texture and leaves no marks.

11- Separate the piece from the mold.

12- Leave the piece to dry slowly. Then, after it has been fired, sand it to make the decorative designs flat and smooth.

13- The finished piece.

Other ideas for modeling with forms

When working with plaster forms, the smooth surface is usually placed over the form. This project uses a different approach: Small pieces of clay that have been previously prepared are arranged inside the mold. They have been made from different-colored clays and shaped into coils, which have been cut into disks.

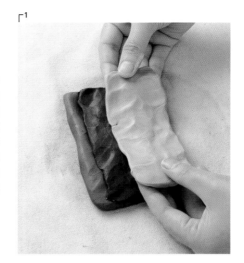

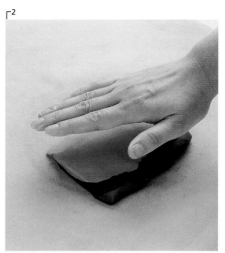

1- Arrange two or three sheets of different-colored clays, one on top of the other, although somewhat separate, to form a spiral.

2- Press both sheets lightly with the hand to bond them together.

3- With the help of the cloth that is being used as a base, roll the sheets.

4- Make a thick colored coil.

5- Use a piece of thread to cut several disks from the coil.

6- Take a concave form and slowly arrange the spiral disks inside it, tapping lightly with your hand. Insert little balls of white clay between the gaps.

7- Brush slip onto the different pieces to help join them together.

8- Clean the piece and smooth it out with your thumbs.

9- Apply a little bit of slip around the rim.

10- Add a coil of white clay on top to give the piece some volume.

11- When the mold is full, use a throwing rib to completely smooth the curved inside surface.

12- Cut off the excess clay from the upper part of the mold.

13

14

13 and 14- Let the piece dry, and when it begins to separate from the mold, remove it completely and smooth out cracks on the outside.

15- Inside and outside view of the finished bowl during the drying process, before it is fired.

15

Ideas for various decorative pieces made with colored clay that can be incorporated into projects.

Simple forms

Balloons and balls can also be used as molds to make round shapes. The balloons can be inflated to the desired volume.

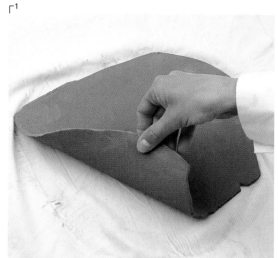

1- Make a slab of clay about 3/16 inches (0.5 mm) thick over a thin cloth base, which can be a piece of an old sheet.

2- On top of the slab, place a balloon blown up to the desired size.

3- Gather all four corners of the cloth, as shown.

4- Tie the corners securely, and twist the cloth that contains the clay and the balloon.

5 and 6- Let the clay stand for a while so that it hardens a little, and then remove the cloth. Any wrinkles, texture, and designs that the cloth has will give the piece an original look. When the cloth has been removed, pop the balloon carefully so the piece does not crack.

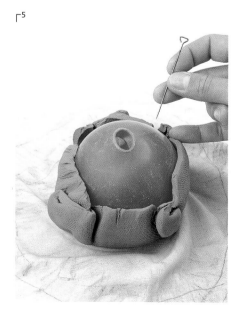

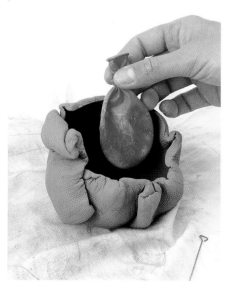

7- The finished piece before it is glazed and baked.

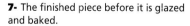

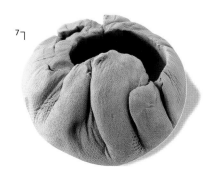

The wheel

Mastery of the potter's wheel requires patience and perseverance without exception. Even potters who are very skilled may need several months of practice before they can throw a piece correctly. For a beginner, it is advisable to attend a throwing class with a competent teacher. Before purchasing a potter's wheel, practice a little so you understand the working process, the appropriate body positions, and the physical conditions that learning how to operate the wheel may entail.

A beautiful vase made on the wheel and decorated with glaze.

Large ceramic pot made on the wheel and decorated by the sculptor Domènec Fita, from the Ceramics series.

Introduction to the wheel

The origin of the potter's wheel dates back to 5000 B.C. It was invented to mass-produce rounded pieces. Through the years the wheel has gone through mechanical changes, which have perfected the way it is operated and added comfort for the person using it. However, the way it works has not changed, thus enabling you to reflect on its shape, its use in throwing clay, its consistency, sanding, the complements, and the recovery of the leftover clay.

Throwing on the wheel requires specific conditions. The clay must have plasticity and should not be too hard. It must be able to stand the water that is added, but at the same time be soft enough not to damage the hands. There is no room in this process for bubbles or lumps of hard or soft clay. Beginners in this craft should resort to ready-made clays, which are moist and prepared for throwing.

How to make a bowl on the wheel

To make a bowl on the wheel, you must first know how to prepare and knead the clay, because it is difficult to throw a piece that has not been properly kneaded. It is also important to learn how to center the pieces, an often difficult task for a beginner.

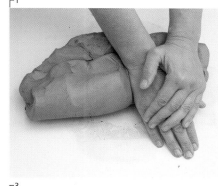

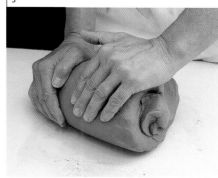

1- To prepare the clay for throwing, knead it thoroughly to remove any air bubbles trapped inside and to ensure that the clay has the same consistency all the way through.

2- Knead the lump of clay with your hands pressing forward. It should not be so soft that it is sticky, or too hard.

3- Keep rolling the lump until it is completely rounded.

4- Shape the kneaded clay into a ball the size of a medium orange. When you have formed several balls, cover them with plastic to keep them moist while you are working on the project.

5- Place the tools that you are going to use near the wheel: a pot with water, a wire to cut the clay, a throwing rib, a serrated blade, a small sponge, a wood board to place the pieces that come off the wheel, and a dish to hold the leftover clay.

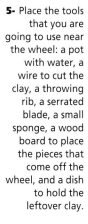

6- Place the lump of clay on the wheel's metal disk, pressing hard on the center, which must be dry.

7- Wet your hands with water, and also apply some to the clay to add moisture.

8- Make the wheel turn counterclockwise, but not too fast at the beginning, pressing with both hands to center the lump of clay.

9 and 10- Keep pressing while you move both hands toward the top. As you move up, reduce the pressure slowly, and let the clay turn while it is completely centered.

11- When your hands reach the top, let them rest motionless while pressing lightly with the thumb to make sure that the clay is still centered.

12- Keep your arms close to your body. Press your thumbs about 1 inch (2.5 cm) into the center of the clay while holding the rest of the lump of clay with your other fingers.

13- Make a slight mark with your middle fingers to define the end of the bowl that you are going to make.

14 and 15- Continue pressing down and flattening to finish the base of the bowl.

16- Now begin marking the bottom. Keep pressing the outside of the clay with the middle finger and the thumb at the point previously defined as the bottom of the bowl.

17 and 18- Place your index finger inside the bowl, and start pressing slowly, holding the wall between two fingers, lifting them together upward. Keep in mind that if you press too hard the bowl will break, and you will have to restart.

19- The second part of shaping the bottom involves completely changing the position of the fingers: Hold the base of the bowl with all the fingers of your left hand, and press the bottom lightly.

20- When you begin to raise the wall, form a hook with your hand to continue pressing. The index and middle fingers are the ones that apply the most pressure.

21- Press the outside wall with your right hand, making a hook with your index finger while your thumb rests next to it touching it.

22- Keep both hands parallel to each other at all times, pressing lightly while raising them to thin the walls.

23- Before you give the piece its final shape, apply slip to the inside and the outside.

24- When the bowl is finished, check the rim with your index finger to make sure it is completely straight.

Modifying the shape of pieces formed on the wheel

When the piece is finished, one of two techniques can be used to modify its shape. One is tapping, and the other involves simply altering the piece using light pressure. Just as soft clay is different from clay that is leather hard, the techniques used to modify their shapes are also different.

From a traditional point of view, modifying a piece that has just been formed on the wheel is a normal practice. A clear example of this is the elongation of a bottleneck or the spout of a pitcher, even though these characteristics may be purely functional. The rims of pieces can also be altered by pinching, or by tapping or pressing on the clay.

Pitchers with spouts made on the wheel, in the process of drying before the handle is added.

The wheel not only allows the mass production of pieces but also can be used to modify the shape of cylindrical objects to make decorative forms with them, such as these made by Jaume Poma, from the series Decorative Ceramics.

Spouts

The spout shape is the one most commonly used in functional pottery. In the old days, a spout was formed at the rim of all water and wine pitchers before taking them off the wheel.

Once the turning of the piece has been finished, the spout is formed before taking the piece off the wheel.

Square shapes

To be able to know how the piece is going to respond after it has been modified, it is important to know the thickness of the wall and the shape that you are starting with. Modifying the piece is not simply reduced to a single tap, slow and firm movements must also be added to deepen and widen the shape.

A couple of wooden sticks can be used to modify the shape of a bowl to make it square. Keep pressing one side and then the other, alternating, until the desired shape is achieved.

Triangular shapes

Triangular shapes can be made easily. A single movement of the thumbs, as if they were a third hand, may be all that is needed.

Place the hands, as shown in the picture, to make triangular shapes.

Modifying the rim

The rim of the piece can be shaped in numerous ways depending on the creative mood of the artist. Many of the possibilities are predetermined by the initial form of the object. Relatively thick walls (more than 3/8 inches [1cm]) can be thinned, and thin borders can be folded or pinched.

Forming pinched shapes is very easy. First make an indentation with your index finger.

Then, make a pinch mark at that point with your thumb and index fingers.

Modifying with tools

The best time to alter the shape of a piece is when the clay is still very soft, which is right after throwing. Under these conditions, and especially with open shapes where some changes have already taken place around the rim and on the walls, the piece may lose some of its original shape. This can be corrected by applying light pressure to the base.

Any object or tool can be used for decorating. In this case a wooden tool is used to make small indentations.

Round objects can be used as well—for example, a piece of fruit, such as a pear, can produce original results.

Cutting facets

Cutting facets is a decorative technique that involves creating a number of flat walls around an object that has already been formed. In the field of ceramics, the carving or the cutting of facets has a much wider significance because many of these pieces could have been produced using different techniques: slabs, molds, or the wheel, arriving at the desired shape afterward by tapping on the object.

The pieces that best respond to cutting facets are those made on the wheel.

This technique requires thicker-than-normal walls, otherwise it would be difficult to cut the facets. The exact thickness required depends on the type of facets that one wishes to make.

1- Cutting with a wire can be done when the piece is still soft. It can be cut from top to bottom or from bottom to top.

2- After the facets are cut, they are smoothed with a flat tool.

Channel decoration

Channels are the parallel grooves that partially or entirely cover the surface of a piece. The grooves can run vertically, diagonally, or horizontally. The channels are given cylindrical shapes on a more spontaneous manner.

When the pieces have concave or convex areas, the grooved sections change according to their height. If you want to channel the entire piece, the spacing between the grooves must conform to the irregular shape of the surface. To use this decorative technique, the walls of the piece must be thicker than normal.

1- Make sure the design is clearly defined before you begin working the clay.

2- Cut a template of the most suitable design, to give you an idea of how the piece will look when it is finished.

3- Draw with a graver or needle on the wet clay.

4- Use a metal tool to carve away the clay and to leave the drawing as a relief.

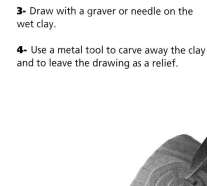

Molds

Working with molds allows you to make similar pieces quickly. Molds have many applications in ceramics because they are made from a porous material that perfectly absorbs the clay's water. The three types of molds for making pottery are press molds, slip molds, and die molds. In this book, only the first two molds are covered because they respond better to decorative applications.

Press molds

Press molds are relatively easy to make. The first step is to choose the model or to create one yourself. It can be made of clay, plastic, or any other material. However, the mold should be simple, and it should not have many nooks and crannies so it can come off easily.

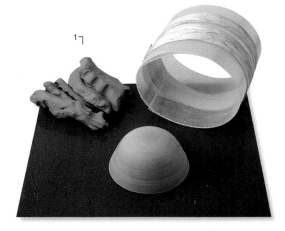

1- First, find a flat, perfectly smooth surface. Place the model that you wish to reproduce in the middle face down.

2- Use a hard plastic to form the walls. Spread soft clay over all surfaces through which the plaster could seep.

3- Apply a releasing agent over the whole structure, making sure that all the surfaces are well covered. Use a sponge to remove any excess. You can find releasing agent in any specialized store. If the agent is a plastic soap, dissolve it in water at a proportion of 1 pound (1/2 kg) of soap to 2 quarts (2 L) water, and bring it to a boil.

4- Next, prepare the plaster of paris: In a bucket filled with water begin incorporating the plaster powder in a constant and even way until it is saturated.

5- Wait until the last layer of plaster is completely wet, and begin to mix it with one hand.

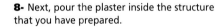

6- Stir with circular motions until all lumps have disappeared.

7- Stop stirring when you feel resistance from the mixture, and tap the bottom of the bucket to release the air bubbles trapped in the plaster. These bubbles could weaken the mold.

8- Next, pour the plaster inside the structure that you have prepared.

9- Tap around the mold again to release any air bubbles that may have formed inside.

10- The plaster sets and heats up fast. This is the signal that in four to five minutes the mold can be removed.

12- Now make a thick bowl on the wheel, following the procedure explained in the chapter "The Wheel" to make the concave model.

13- When the bowl is completely dry, pour the plaster mixture into it.

11- Release the convex model from the mold, wiping inside with a wet sponge to clean it. Let it dry.

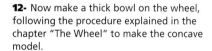

14- Pour the plaster until it reaches slightly above the rim, and then tap the mold lightly to release any air bubbles.

15- Make a few notches in the mold so you can grab it easily when the plaster dries, and then let it set.

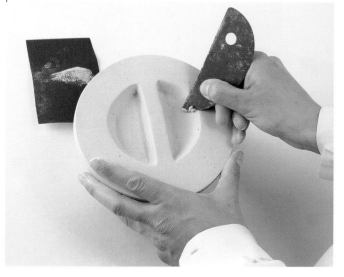

Slip molds

Slip casting is faster than the wheel for mass-producing ceramic pieces. It is the system used by small factories to mass-produce identical pieces. Liquid clay or slip is poured into the mold. The mixture is made with the following proportions: 11 pounds (5 kg) powdered porcelain clay to 2 quarts (2 L) water to 1 tsp (5 g) sodium carbonate to 2 tsp (10 g) sodium silicate.

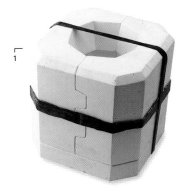

1- Assemble the mold and hold it together with a rubber band, as shown in the picture.

2- Prepare the clay as explained before, and pour it into the mold.

3- Let it stand for 15 minutes, and then tilt the mold to remove the piece. It should remain inverted for about 45 minutes. The time is given as a guide, because each mold and each piece are different.

4 and 5- Remove the rim of the mold with a tool, trying not to damage it.

6- Now remove the rubber bands, and open the mold.

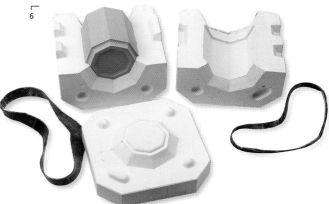

7- Release the resulting cast carefully and vertically, to avoid causing any damage.

8- Trim off the edges, and leave the piece to leather dry. After that, decorate it any way you want.

chapter

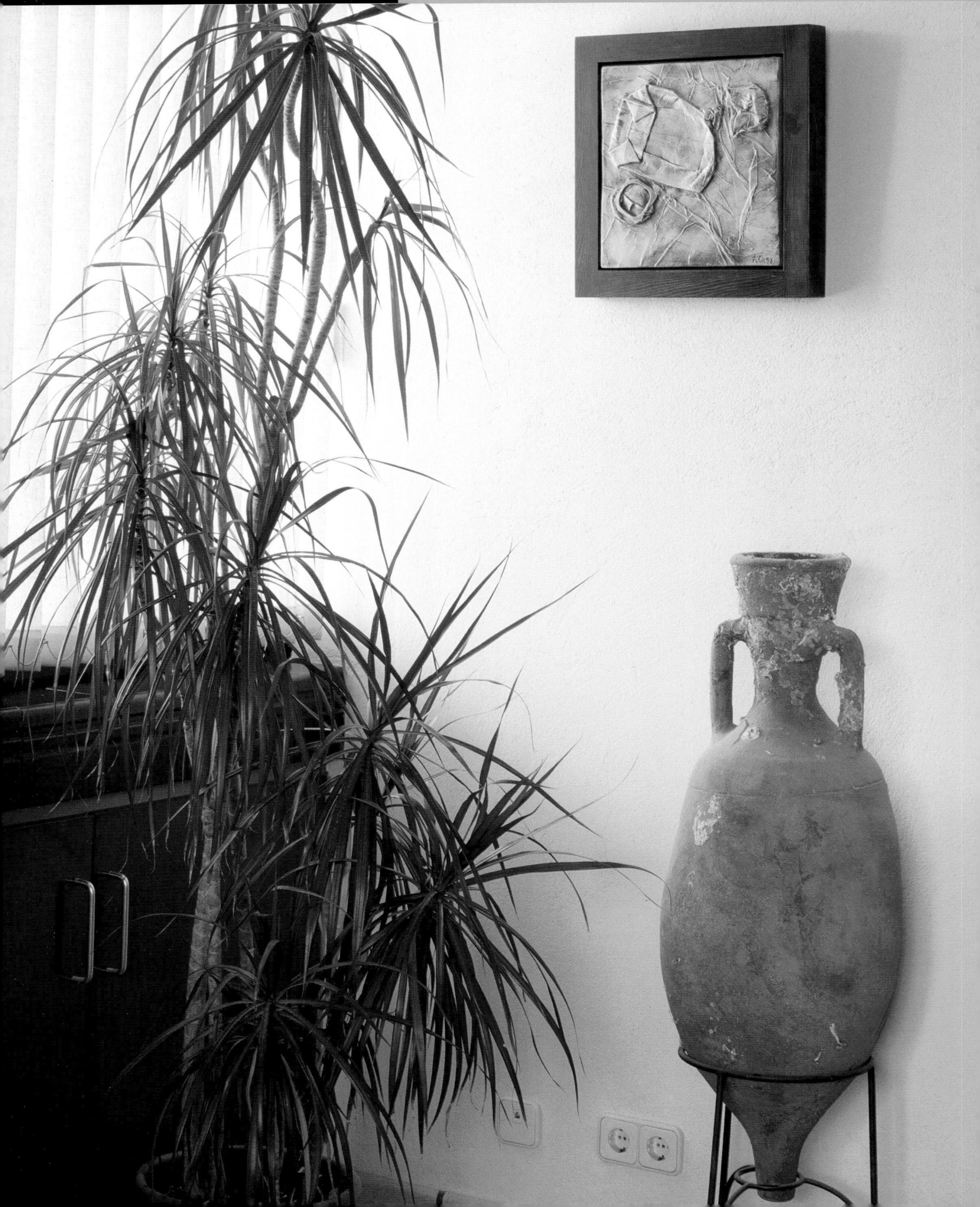

Decorating techniques

This chapter covers the most commonly used decorative techniques for low-fire clays in soft or leather hard conditions. Special attention is given to procedures that do not require mechanical devices or special tools, so that anyone can obtain satisfactory results, without many tools.

This chapter is divided into two large groups: "Impressions, texture, and relief" and "Perforations, inlay, and stamped impressions." Each section presents a different process, with slight variations, illustrated with a series of photographs that explain the process.

Impressions, texture, and relief

Because of its plasticity, clay can be used for engraving, texturing, or marking with impressions and relief. It can be modeled and formed into any shape or form, depending on how creative the artist is. It is easy to get excited at the prospect of the endless decorative possibilities, which can be applied to clay objects that are soft or leather hard.

Sculpture piece made with refractory clay. Work by Madola from the Doors series.

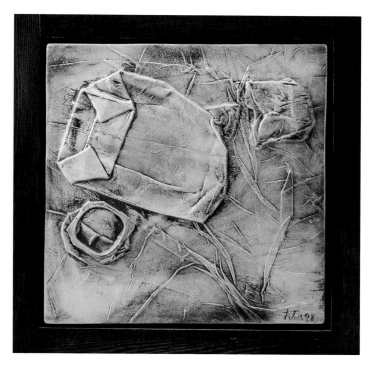

Piece with relief made from inlaid textures and decorated with oxides. Work by Domènec Fita from the Ceramics series.

Original piece modeled from slabs and decorated with different engraving techniques. Work by Andicona Aristondo.

Scratching and incisions

Although there is no clear defining line between scratching and incising, scratching is almost always used to describe a broader and deeper relief than the marks associated with incising.

Clay is such an easy material to cut that scratching it presents no difficulty. The quality of the mark or of the surface produced depends as much on the moisture or dryness of the clay as on the tools used. In practice, scratching is not usually done on soft clay because it tends to stick to the tool. Most scratching is done when the clay has dried leather hard, which is when it can be easily cut, offering no resistance to the tools. Scratching presents very few technical problems. It is obvious that piercing the wall must be avoided in hollow shapes. Scratch marks must be delicate and shallow. The required tools are not necessarily the specific ones used for piercing or for similar techniques. Any object that can perform the tasks of cutting, scraping, or engraving can be used—for example, wires, metal or wooden instruments, or sticks.

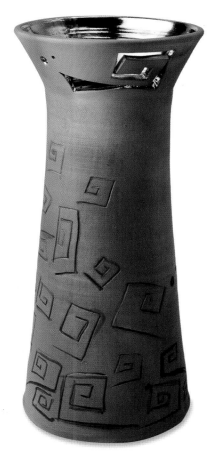

Artistic vase made on the wheel and later decorated with scratching and incising.

Texture on clay that is still soft

The quality of the impressions on the surface of the piece depends as much on the moisture or dryness of the clay as on the tools that are used. Therefore an endless array of decorative effects can be produced.

Relief motifs can be made on pottery pieces using various pointed objects, including those devised by the artist, such as recycled or discarded objects found around the house or at the recycling center.

Simple decorations and textures that are easy to apply to clay can also be made by using common organic materials, such as leaves, bark, twigs, grains, wood shavings, and grass. Almost any object that has a textured surface can be used to create a design.

When choosing your materials, keep in mind the depth of the relief, the effects, and the design that they may produce. Then, place these materials on a recently made slab of clay or object, pressing as soft or as hard as you wish, to make the decoration.

The following pages illustrate the wide variety of decorative results that you can produce with engravings and textures using different tools and materials.

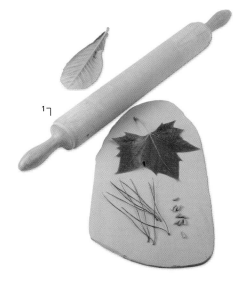

1- This piece uses organic materials, such as leaves, twigs, and tree roots. They have been arranged on the sheet of soft clay, forming a decorative design.

2- When the placement of the pieces has been finalized, they are pressed lightly by rolling the pin over them very slowly.

When the texture is finished, a mural of different dimensions can be made, always playing with the repetition of motifs.

Any color or type of clay can be used. The subtlety of the decorative effect depends on the depth of the texture of the chosen objects and on the finish applied to the piece.

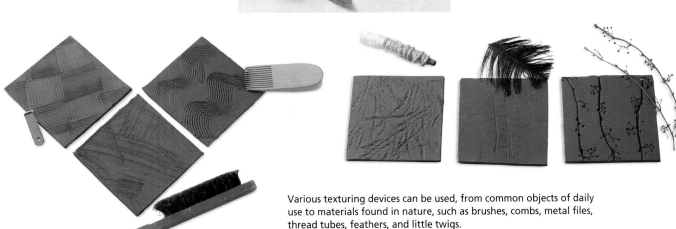

Various texturing devices can be used, from common objects of daily use to materials found in nature, such as brushes, combs, metal files, thread tubes, feathers, and little twigs.

It is easier to print textures on flat surfaces, because a rolling pin can be used to make deep impressions. When the marks have been made, the pieces acquire interesting effects and offer many possibilities for the application of color.

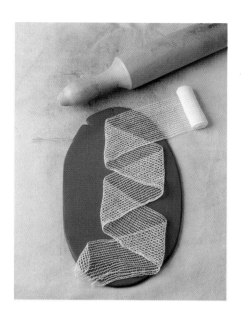

A day at the beach is also a good opportunity to think about collecting shells and objects that are found in the sand.

Thread has diverse applications. Here, it produces excellent results.

Metal construction rods can make interesting designs that are difficult to produce with any other tool.

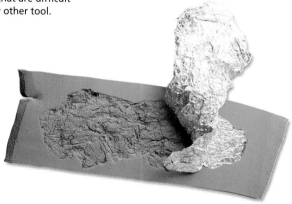

Aluminum paper also has great decorative value.

The ideas that come to mind for making incisions on clay are endless, and the list could go on and on.

Impressing on leather hard clay

Clay that has dried leather hard can be decorated using a tapping and pressing technique. This is mainly done with wooden implements that have a wide base. Working with leather hard clay always takes longer than working with soft clays; however, firm clay does allow for greater control and precision.

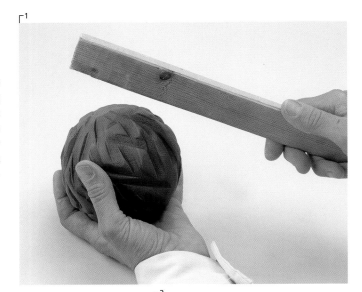

1- Form a ball of clay, and let it dry leather hard. Then tap it with a piece of wood for an interesting effect.

2- Let the clay dry a bit more. Cut it with a thread, and hollow it out to turn it into a box.

3- Empty both halves carefully, constantly checking the thickness of the walls.

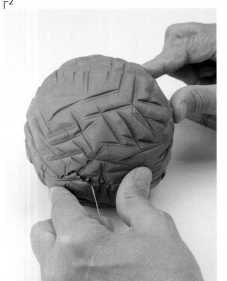

4- When you are finished emptying them and the walls are even, scrape the inside with a hollowing tool until it is completely smooth.

5- Finish smoothing the inside with a wooden tool, and put both halves together aside to dry.

6- View of the finished piece, glazed and baked.

Impressing on plaster or on press molds

Impressing on plaster normally saves a lot of work, especially if a number of pieces have to be made. Plaster is a wonderful material for engraving because marking it with a sharp tool is easy. The technique is called press molding. Press molds are essential for reproducing designs on slabs that must be repeated many times, because you can achieve delicate effects by pressing the clay lightly over them, thus producing very decorative details.

1- Make a border on a sheet of plaster, making sure that the lines are deep enough.

2- If you want to make murals with a specific texture or design using this technique, place a slab of clay at the bottom of the mold, applying light pressure to get an impression of the mold's motif. When you separate the sheet from the mold, you will have the relief of the decoration that you had made on the plaster.

3- It is very important to let the molds dry properly. Any of these designs would be good for making a repeated border.

4- Choose one of the motifs to make a border. Make a slab of clay with the rolling pin, cut the clay according to the size of the mold that you wish to use, and fit it in the mold.

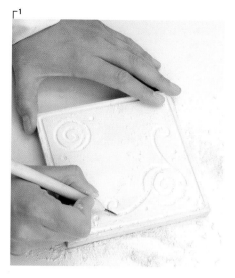

5- Press the slab with your fingers, making sure that all nooks and crannies are properly filled.

6- Clean the surface with a throwing rib to make it completely smooth. Let it dry, at which time the piece will separate by itself.

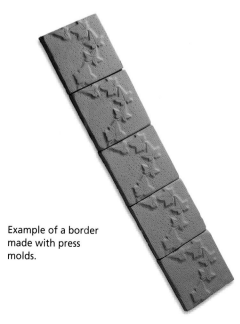

Example of a border made with press molds.

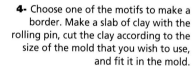

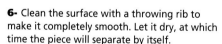

Decorating with relief

There is a long tradition in the history of ceramics of working with modeling techniques. The pieces can be made using coils formed on the potter's wheel or using molds. It is impossible to separate the modeling process from decorating with relief in handmade pieces, which is why this technique is considered part of the modeling phase, instead of a separate procedure that is applied to a piece that is already finished.

Added relief

Creating a relief on the surface of a piece involves manipulating the clay with your fingers or with the appropriate tools, such as sticks or knives. From the technical standpoint of this exercise, two things must be kept in mind: First, the added clay must adhere to the walls of the piece properly so it does not break or come loose when it is drying or being baked. Second, the relief must not be so big, heavy, or thick that it may cause problems at the time of baking. You can avoid both problems by simply working on the modeling while the clay is still soft. However, it is not necessary to finish the modeling right after making the piece. Detailed work should be done when the clay has dried leather hard. The simplest decorative motifs are small, soft clay reliefs that can be applied to the surface, as long as the clay has not surpassed the leather dry stage. It is helpful to use a little bit of slip as a bonding agent.

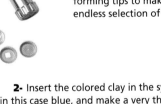

1- You can make relief designs by using the simplest imaginable devices—for example, a special metal syringe for clay, which you can purchase with many forming tips to make an endless selection of motifs.

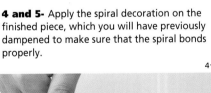

2- Insert the colored clay in the syringe, in this case blue, and make a very thin coil.

3- Roll the coil in the shape of a spiral. This must be done quickly to prevent the coil from hardening and breaking.

4 and 5- Apply the spiral decoration on the finished piece, which you will have previously dampened to make sure that the spiral bonds properly.

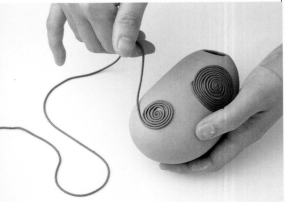

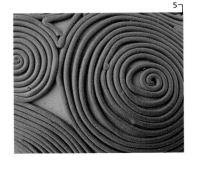

6- View of the finished relief.

Making raised decorations with a sprig mold

Applying molded decorations to the surface of a piece requires two processes: first, creating the mold; second, making the clay decorations and applying them to the surface of the piece. The major advantages of this technique are the ability to produce numerous decorations from the same mold and the delicate and exact quality of the work. An added advantage is the ability to make the decorations in a color different from that of the base. Although applying decoartions that protrude too much can be difficult, covering the piece with smaller decorations is relatively easy.

1- The first step in making raised motifs is creating the model. Once the design is decided, the model can be made with any type of clay that is available. In this case, red clay is used to make a simple star.

2- Next, the model is made. First arrange four wood pieces, securing them with pads of soft clay to prevent the plaster from seeping through the corners. Place the model in the center, a bit damp, to make sure it stays in place so that the plaster does not seep underneath.

3- After making sure that everything is perfectly arranged, slowly pour the plaster.

4- Tap the mold gently to release any air bubbles that may have formed.

5- Remove any excess plaster with a ruler or other similar device, when it has acquired a little more consistency.

6- Finish removing the excess plaster with a metal throwing rib or similar tool, working from the center to the sides to leave the surface of the mold completely smooth.

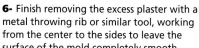

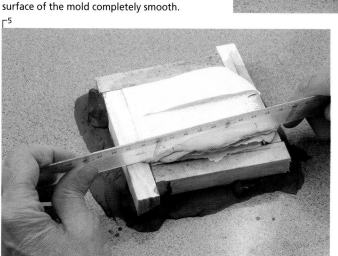

7- Wait a few minutes until the plaster hardens, at which time the edges can be rounded and the mold cleaned.

8- The mold is now finished. Continue by making the relief motifs that you need for decorating the piece. Place clay in the mold, and pack it with your fingers.

9- Flatten and scrape from the center out with any object that has a flat side.

10- A scraping movement from the center outward packs the clay against the borders of the mold, producing a well-defined impression, whereas a simple movement from edge to edge tends to release the motif from the mold.

11- When the motif is completely flat, place a piece of wet clay on top of it, pressing lightly. This will stick to the motif and make its removal from the mold easier.

Attaching molded designs to the piece

Applying clay motifs in different colors can help provide visual interest. However, extra care must be taken to prevent the color from staining the piece.

1- Attaching the molded decorations to the piece is easy. First, scratch the surface with a sharp tool, before putting the design in place.

2- Brush it with a little bit of water, which will act as a bonding agent.

3- Then paint the motif with water or slip.

4- When you are finished with this step, attach the pieces together with a circular motion, applying light pressure.

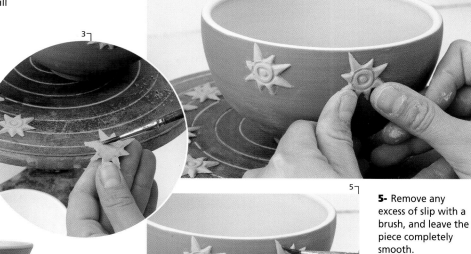

5- Remove any excess of slip with a brush, and leave the piece completely smooth.

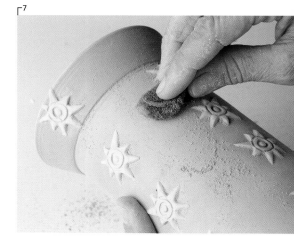

6- Motifs can be applied to any piece and made from any color that you like.

7- When the piece is dry, rub it with a steel wool pad to make it completely smooth before putting it in the kiln to be fired.

Perforations, inlay, and stamped impressions

This section includes three completely different decorative techniques. The goal of each is to obtain a different result each time. Perforation is a technique that always fluctuates between freedom and precision and between creative shapes and geometric formality, showing that pottery is more than a method of creating containers or other functional objects.

A large ceramic vase decorated with stamps and with some designs painted with oxides.

Piece decorated with inlays of different colored clays. Work by Albert Viladrosa.

Perforations

As the name indicates, perforation involves decorating a piece by cutting through its walls. Although perforating a piece clearly limits its functionality, the intent may be functional, semifunctional, or purely decorative. Regardless of why the perforations are used, the visual possibilities created with this technique must take into account the thickness of the wall, as well as the visual field revealed by the perforation.

If you have to perforate very thin walls or if you want to make holes on sides that are not straight, you will need a tool with a very fine point. You can use a properly sharpened piece of hacksaw blade.

1- First, outline the areas that you want to cut with a pencil or with a needle. Even if you have a sharp tool, if you are working with thin walls, it is better to pierce an initial hole and to keep enlarging it until you get the desired size.

2- In all perforating jobs, the areas that protrude the most tend to break easily. To prevent this from happening, you must cut from those areas in. You can use a special tool, like a hollow tube, to make smaller holes.

3- Even if you have a very fine tool, when you are working with thin walls, it is preferable to hold the clay that you are cutting with one hand positioned on the inside, while cutting with the other.

4- The cutting edges are an inherent danger of this process. However, sometimes it is necessary to remove small pieces of clay that have become lodged onto the cut surface and around the edges. To do this, wait until the piece is completely dry, and then rub the surface with a piece of steel wool, until the edge is rounded and smooth.

5- Allow the piece to dry completely before it is baked.

Inlays in soft clays

Inlay refers to the process of filling the lines or the grooves of a piece with a similar material but of different color, to produce a smooth surface where the lines or the designs stand out for their color.

When inlay is applied to an object, special care must be taken to ensure that all the clays have the same consistency, preferably soft.

Before starting with the inlay process, the depth of the line or groove must be decided, and the clays must be properly chosen according to the colors that are needed to make the design previously selected or drawn on paper.

The grooves can be made by applying an impression or by removing the clay directly from the piece. The grooves must be somewhat deep so the designs do not get distorted with the pressure that is applied on the clay.

1- Begin by making a drawing or a model on paper to help you visualize the final result.

2- First, draw the lines with a pencil on the leather hard piece.

3- Then, cut out the lines with a hollowing tool. Remove the clay from all the lines with a steady hand until you get somewhat deep grooves.

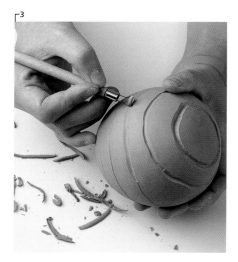

4- Before the colored clay is applied, deepen the grooves with a sharper tool to promote the bonding of both clays.

5- The piece should be soft. If it has dried, apply a little bit of water with a sprayer before you begin inlaying.

6- The clay that you intend to inlay must also be soft. Make thin coils and begin inserting them in the grooves, pressing lightly. If the piece gets dirty, you can clean it later.

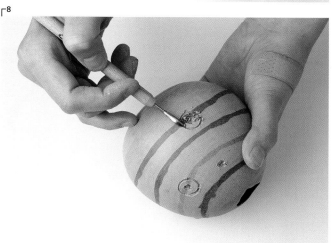

7- After clay has been inserted in all grooves, remove the clay that bulges out with a metal throwing rib, until the piece is completely clean. This is the most common technique for making the larger inlaid areas flush. The scraping motions should be precise, delicate, and unhurried.

8- You can inlay over inlays with clays of different colors. To do this, first make the grooves as explained before.

9- Then begin inserting the different colored clay in all the grooves.

10- Scrape the excess clay with a throwing rib to view the results.

11- When the piece is completely clean and decorated, set it aside.

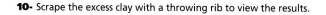

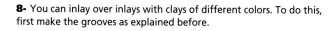

Inlays combined with relief

When referring to inlays combined with relief, one begins to see the great decorative possibilities that the world of ceramics offers, where several techniques can be combined in one piece. To an object decorated with markings filled with colored clay, decorations made with a mold have been added and bonded to the surface of the piece when the clay is still leather hard. It is interesting to observe the numerous possibilities of this technique. There are endless options, working with colored clays alone.

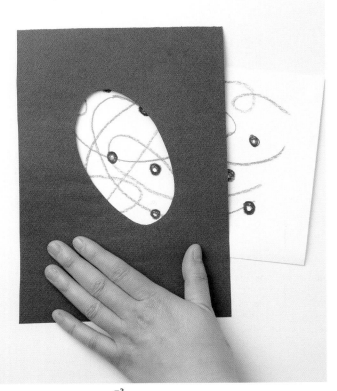

1- It is important to begin by establishing the design for the project. First, draw the decorative motifs on a piece of white paper. Then cut a piece of cardboard or construction paper to simulate the shape of the piece, and try different positions to find the most appropriate layout.

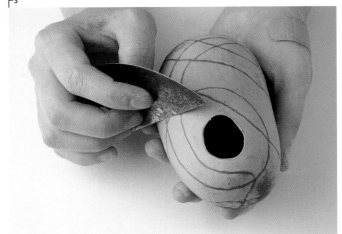

2- Begin inlaying by following the process explained in the previous exercise. Draw the lines and make the incisions, and begin inserting the colored clay.

3- Then, scrape the excess clay with a metal throwing rib. The final cleaning is done when the piece is completely dry, rubbing with a piece of steel wool. Make sure you remove the fine dust formed during this process. You can also clean the piece with sandpaper in its bisque state, when the decoration is completely exposed.

4- Next, make the raised motifs with a mold, following the process already described (see page 71).

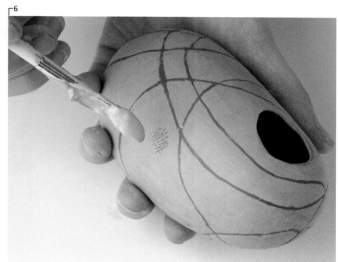

5- Making the sprig mold is very easy when the motifs are small. Put all the pieces together on a flat surface, making sure they are properly attached to the base. If necessary, they can be dampened lightly. Make a small wall of clay around the pieces, either round or rectangular in shape. Prepare the plaster separately, and when it is relatively thick pour it inside the confines of the clay to make the mold. When the plaster is dry, release the forms from the mold following the usual process.

6- Use slip to attach the relief pieces. After scratching the piece to be decorated, apply a little bit of clay to the areas where the motifs are going to be placed.

7- Then, apply slip to the base of the motif, and paint the top of the piece with slip as well.

8- Finally, attach each motif to the piece.

9- By combining different decorative techniques in one piece, the process is more creative—and more enjoyable.

Impressing with stamps

The purpose of impressing clay with stamps is to highlight the shape in such way that the result is visually balanced. Impressing with stamps completes the form, but it is important to keep in mind the method used for forming the piece. Working with stamps is easier with objects made using coils or slabs, and with pieces formed on the potter's wheel. Basically, there are two types of impressing stamps: flat and convex.

Flat stamps are those that can be pressed directly onto the clay, making an impression right away. The consistency or hardness of the clay must be checked before pressure is applied on the stamps. Because it is difficult to make an impression if the piece is too hard, in this case, the piece should be dampened or soft clay applied to the area that is to be decorated.

Convex stamps include those that are applied on the clay with a light rolling motion. It is not necessary to press too hard, because only a small portion of the stamp makes contact with the piece. Simply keep in mind that the softer the clay is the easier it is to make a clean impression.

The relief does not have to consist of groupings of flat and indented areas: It can be a three-dimensional impression. However, before you take the first step, it is a good idea to plan the type of decoration that you want to achieve and to do some testing on a sheet of clay before deciding.

Detail of a decoration with stamps on a vase.

Samples of rounded and flat stamps, shown with the tools used to make them.

How to make stamps

Although you can use any material to make stamps, the most appropriate and recommended ones are plaster and baked clay. Because they are highly porous, they tend to separate easily from the clay, leaving a clean form or impression. When a stamp begins to stick or does not come off properly, it must be cleaned and covered with talcum powder to prevent the problem from recurring.

Stamps made with nonporous materials, such as metal, usually do not produce clean impressions on hard clay, and then they begin to stick. In general, metal should not be used on soft clay. There are several ways to prevent nonporous stamps from sticking to the clay. Deciding which one to use depends basically on the complexity of the stamp and the consistency of the clay. The two most common are the application of talcum powder to the area of the clay that you want to stamp and the lubrication of the surface of the stamp with a cloth soaked in oil. When the stamps are made of clay, they are easier to use if they are baked at lower-than-normal temperatures so that they continue to have a high degree of porosity and release from the base easily.

1- First, form a piece of clay in the shape of a coil, and then cut it down to a manageable size. You can make the coil square or round, depending on the stamp you want to create.

2- You can use any object at hand to make the incisions—for example, a pencil. Press it lightly onto the clay until you get the desired impression.

3- You can use the point of the same pencil to make other types of smaller incisions.

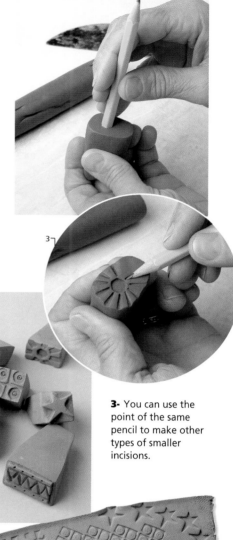

4- Let the stamp dry completely, and then bake it at a lower-than-normal temperature—for example 1,492°F (800°C)—so that it maintains its porosity.

5- Before using the stamp on a piece, test it on a scrap of clay, because once the impression is applied it is difficult to erase.

6- When you are sure about the stamp, begin decorating the piece. In this case, it is a tray made and a pressed mold.

You can also decorate coils, which when baked can be used as convex stamps. The picture shows a decorative design made with a plastic object.

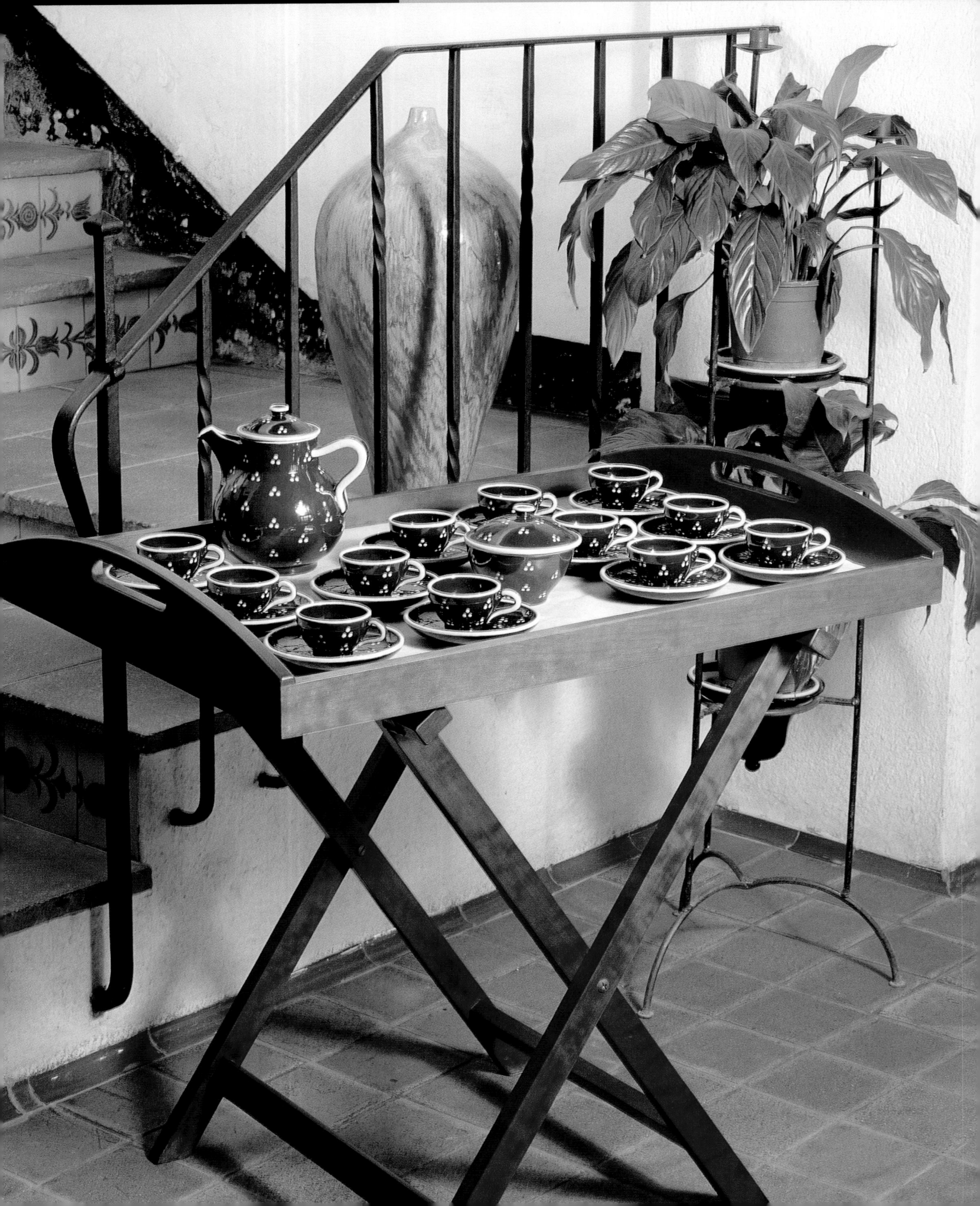

Engobes

In the history of ceramics, engobes make their appearance much earlier than glazes. They were commonly used by the Egyptians, the Greeks, and the Romans, and they spread to England and all over Europe during the eighteenth century.

Engobes consist of a liquid clay, usually colored, and are typically used to correct defects in the clay. The techniques associated with their use are also used for drawing, painting, and decorating ceramic pieces. The engobes that are still used by some indigenous cultures are made of natural clays or metal oxides. They produce incredible pieces, most of the time simply burnishing them with a stone or with a very fine tool when the clay is leather hard. This chapter covers all the aspects of the techniques used for decorating with engobes.

Working with engobes

Working with engobes is one of the most versatile techniques in the field of ceramics. A person can chose from a variety of possibilities, either from the ones explained in this chapter or from those learned while practicing the craft in the shop.

In some instances, engobe is also referred to as slip, but there is a slight difference between them.

Plate decorated with a black engobe base, and later decorated with white engobe applied using a slip trailer. Work by Vila-Clara.

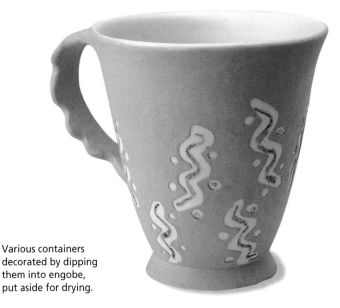

Pitcher made with stencils and decorated with colored engobe applied with a brush. Work by Yukiko Murata.

Various containers decorated by dipping them into engobe, put aside for drying.

Technical characteristics of engobes

An engobe is a clay that is applied over another clay that contracts at its same rate. Engobes can be found in nature, or they can be prepared using a good quality white clay that has quite a bit of plasticity. It is applied on leather-hard pieces—that is, when the pieces are still damp and have a moist color, but their shape cannot be altered. This technique provides a quality to the piece that no other decorative technique can surpass.

Engobes can also be prepared for dry or bisque pieces; however, the application techniques are not the same. This chapter covers the composition of engobes and the applications of them on single fire and glaze fire. But first, it offers a technical review of the properties of the engobes in general, of the different decorative techniques, and of the application techniques.

Purpose of engobes

In many cultures, engobe is the preferred technique, mostly for technical reasons. For example, when clay is very porous, it absorbs more glaze. If you apply a glaze that is more pure, it will cover the pores and melt better using a smaller amount. In conclusion, when you work with older techniques, more often than not you will find that they originated and were commonly used because of their technical properties.

There are many reasons why engobe is used. Let's look at some of them.

It helps cover pores and imperfections of the clay.

It changes the color of the base clay. For example, a red clay can be turned white, a white one red, and so on.

It helps vitrify the glaze because it is a more pure form of clay and is less porous.

It helps the oxides settle. When pure oxides are used over a dry piece and a thick layer of transparent lead glaze is added to it, the oxides run. To prevent the oxides from running, about 40 percent engobe is added to it.

It helps fix the dyes. When pure dyes are applied without engobe, and a transparent lead glaze is added, the dyes separate. To prevent that from happening, a 20 percent engobe is added to the dyes.

Properties of engobes

Engobe has several properties that must be observed. So special attention should be given to this chapter to make sure the content is clear. The main properties of engobes are plasticity and refractivity.

Plasticity

Clay has the quality of plasticity, which refers to the clay's malleability when wet. The term *plasticity* is related to dilation and contraction. So if you apply a layer of plastic clay over one that is not, you will need to take into account the differences.

While drying, the base clay may shrink more than the layer of engobe, and this can cause the piece to crack or break.

To complement the differences in plasticity between the engobe and the base clay, you must make the plasticity of both the same so that they will dry at the same rate and contract the same way.

How do you know when an engobe has the same dilation rate as the clay? Because it is difficult to judge by appearance, you must experiment. When you begin to apply engobe to a piece that is "leather hard," that is, still fairly soft, and cracks appear when the piece dries out, it means that the contraction rate between the engobe and the clay is different.

Refractivity

The refractivity of the clay is the opposite of plasticity. A refractory compound tends to reduce the contraction of the engobes during the drying process, and the adherence to the base. Quartz, feldspar, alumina, and carbonates are refractory compounds. Engobe should have a certain degree of refractivity and should resist the temperature that the glaze reaches during baking, which is why it must contain plastic and refractory materials.

When the engobe flakes off, it means that there is a difference in refractivity. Either the plasticity of the engobe or the type of clay that is used for the engobe application will have to be corrected.

When the cracks formed resemble fish scale, it means that part of the piece was too dry before the engobe was applied.

Composition

Although the basic component of the engobe is any clay that is white and that has relative plasticity, the engobe must also contain plastic and refractory materials. Clays regulate the plasticity, and quartz, feldspar, and kaolin regulate the refractivity.

In the case of single-fire engobes— that is, those that are applied over damp clays that are leather hard—white clays are used for plasticity so they adhere better to the base clay. Kaolin makes the engobe whiter, and it controls refractivity. Quartz, which also controls the refractivity, is added in small amounts when the base clay and the engobe have very different shrinking proportions, or engobe is used for painting. Keep in mind that if it is applied too thick, cracks will appear. Feldspar is also added sometimes as a refractivity regulator and, because of its melting characteristics, helps in the bonding of the engobe to the piece.

The basic materials for making engobes— clay, kaolin, quartz, and feldspar—all look very similar.

Several engobe formulas

The engobe technique is the one that offers the widest variety of decorative possibilities. It can be used in single-fire mixtures and glaze-fire mixtures, and the results are always good.

Single-firing engobes

There are several formulas for applying single-fire engobes on damp, leather-hard clays. Below are the two most common ones.

Engobe mixture ready to be dissolved in water. When the water has been added, a blender will be used to prevent lumps from forming.

Once the engobe has been prepared, it should be passed through an 80-screen sieve.

	Formula 1	Formula 2
White clay	60%	70%
Kaolin	20%	20%
Feldspar	10%	—
Quartz	10%	10%

After the different components have been mixed and dissolved in water according to the proportions indicated, they must be sifted. An 80-screen sieve is good for engobes. It is a good idea to prepare and store some for later use, to avoid having to mix it every time you need it.

The engobe, which in this case is being applied using a brush with very fine bristles, must have the consistency of a thick puree.

Glaze-firing or vitrifying engobes

The glaze-firing engobes, also called vitrifying engobes, are applied over dry or bisque clay. Because the application techniques are not the same as the ones for single-firing, their formulas are also different. Some melting material must be added to the formula, so when the piece is baked, the engobe will adhere better and not flake off.

Glaze-firing engobes can be applied with a spray gun, a brush, or a sponge, but they should not be applied by dipping. They are used mainly for decorative purposes. The point is for them to become vitrified to the piece without being too noticeable. This will provide good resistance and hardness to the color. The following table shows four possible formulas.

Weighing the basic materials to make an engobe. To guarantee good results, it is important to be precise in the mixture of the chosen formula.

	Formula 1	Formula 2	Formula 3	Formula 4
White clay	62%	50%	18%	25%
Kaolin	—	40%	18%	11%
Feldspar	36%	10%	18%	—
Calcium carbonate	2%	—	—	—
Quartz	—	—	18%	32%
Lead bisilicate	—	—	28%	32%

How to control the density of the engobe

Density refers to the amount of water that must be added to the mixture of engobe to ensure the same coat on the piece every time it is applied. There are different methods to control this factor: using a density gauge, measuring by weight, and estimating the thickness with a brush or with your hand.

The density of the engobe must range between 50 and 60 on the density gauge scale. This density would be appropriate for dipping.

Using a density gauge

This method is ruled by the laws of flotation. When the density gauge is inserted in the container of engobe, it will sink more or less, depending on the density of the mixture. The density gauge has a series of numbers that indicate the density of the engobe, which must be between 50 and 60.

Density gauge used for measuring the density of the engobes and glazes.

Estimating with a brush

When you need a small amount of engobe, a brush can be used to make an estimate, as shown below.

1- After mixing the engobe, insert into it the brush that you are going to use for painting, and lift it out very slowly. If it drips a lot, then the engobe has too much water. To fix, remove some of the water and allow it to sit.

2- Repeat. If the brush does not drip when lifted, the engobe is too thick. To fix, add water.

3- When the brush has a drop on it but barely drips, the density of the engobe is correct for application to the piece.

Measuring by weight

The density of the engobe can also be measured by weight. If you mix 60 percent water and 40 percent engobe, you will get perfect density, but you must take the following precautions. The container must be covered properly because when the water begins to evaporate, the density will change drastically. This method is good the first time you prepare the engobe, but after several days using it, you will have to resort to an easier and more reliable system.

To get the perfect density, the base materials and the water must be added in precise amounts.

Estimating with a hand

When you need a large quantity of engobe that will be applied for dipping, you may use a different system, also approximate, to see if the density of the engobe is correct. This consists of testing it with one hand.

1- Insert a hand in the container, and mix the engobe thoroughly until it acquires the same consistency all the way through. This procedure requires at least 5 minutes.

2- When the material is mixed well, pull your hand out slowly. If it is completely covered and looks as if you are wearing a glove, without drips from the tips of the fingers, the engobe is the right density.

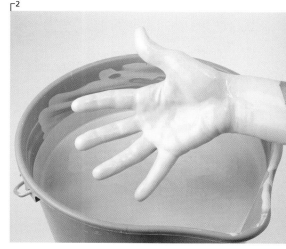

3- Now another example. This time, if your hand comes out of the mixture relatively transparent, and you can see the color of the skin, that means that there is too much water. You must remove some water and let it rest until the next day.

4- Repeat. If you notice that your hand is heavy when you lift it from the mixture, and the tips of the fingers are about to drip, that means it needs a little water, which you can add immediately and mix again.

Applying single-fire engobes

One of the most complicated aspects of handling the engobe is application. No matter what process is chosen, the density of the engobe is the key factor.

Engobe can be applied by dipping, with a brush or sponge, or with a spray gun. The method most often used for artistic pottery is dipping.

In any case, engobe must be properly prepared with water, and the density must be measured with one of the previously explained methods, before application.

When the engobe has been applied to the piece according to your specifications, you will not need to do anything to it until it completely dries.

Dipping

Engobes are usually applied using a dipping process. When a piece is dipped in engobe, two factors will establish the right time and conditions for applying it correctly: the engobe must be the right consistency, and the piece must be leather hard. It cannot be too dry, otherwise the engobe will flake off like fish scale.

1- First, pour the engobe inside the piece, so the piece will stay moist until the next day.

2- Pour the engobe out of the container, trying not to stain the outside too much.

3- Next, apply the engobe to the upper half of the piece, and leave it to dry until it has acquired a leathery consistency so that the piece can be handled.

4- The process of applying engobe by halves is used for any kind of piece.

5 and 6- The next day, when the engobe that has been applied already is leather hard, and can be handled, dip the bottom half. Then allow the piece to completely dry. This method for applying engobe makes it possible for the piece to be handled without leaving fingerprints all over it.

7- When the piece has been completely covered with engobe, put it aside until it has dried out completely.

Application with a brush

To apply engobe with a brush, you must know exactly what type and size of brush to use. It is better to apply it using a wide brush with very fine hair, because the brushstrokes are less visible, and the final result is better.

1- To apply engobe with a brush, the mixture should be much thicker than for dipping. Its texture should be similar to a thick puree. If it is not, the pieces that come out of the kiln will look like they have no engobe.

2- When applying the engobe with a wide brush, it is important to stroke it freely.

3- This method of applying engobe is very slow. The brushing is done after the previous coat has dried out a little.

4- At the end, almost always, the transparency of the brushstrokes is left as decoration.

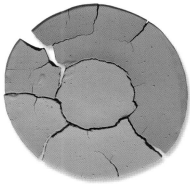

If the piece is covered with too much engobe, or if it is fully dipped, the result can be disastrous. You must never forget that the single-fire engobes are applied when the pieces are still damp.

It is difficult to apply engobe with a brush without leaving visible brush marks. Because the piece is damp, it does not absorb the water, and so it is much more difficult for the engobe to stick to the piece. Therefore you will have to take advantage of the transparent brushstroke and use it as a decorative feature.

Applying texture with a brush

Applying engobe with a brush can produce an endless number of decorative effects. Most of the pieces that have a textured surface present the opportunity to create special effects when the clay is wet. When the engobe is applied with a brush, the result will vary greatly if different elements and textures are used.

1 and 2- After the piece has been painted, scrape it with any object at hand—for example, a brush with coarse bristles.

3 and 4- Before applying the engobe, you can place a piece of fabric on top of the piece—in this case gauze—to be used as a pattern.

5 and 6- After applying the engobe, remove the fabric. The result will be a piece with both engobe and texture.

7 and 8- You can finish the piece with other decorative techniques, or you can simply leave it as is, ready for glazing.

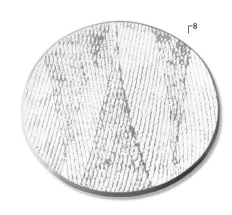

Applying engobe with a sponge

The sponge is an excellent tool for applying engobe, because it is easier to apply a thicker layer than with a brush, and therefore be able to completely cover the piece.

2- Apply several coats, one on top of the other, after letting each one dry.

1- Soak the sponge with white engobe, and apply it on the piece, trying not to drag it.

3- The piece is wet, so you do not want to touch it with your hands. Use two tiles, for example, to invert it. Put it aside to dry completely so that it can be decorated.

Applying engobe with a spray gun

Applying engobe with a spray gun is rarely used for pieces that are damp or leather hard, because such pieces cannot absorb the water from the engobe, and persistence is necessary for achiecing the desired thickness. In most cases this is a difficult task. The most common thickness for an engobe is 1/50 inch (0.5 mm). However, it is not impossible to apply engobe with a spray gun: It is just complicated and requires much more time.

On the other hand, applying engobe with a gun is an excellent choice for glaze-fire pieces. When the piece is bisque, it absorbs water easily, and you can apply the layer that you want, keeping in mind that the thickness of the engobe must be about 1/50 inch (0.5 mm).

1- Applying engobe with a spray gun is a slow process because several layers are required.

2- Begin with the top part, and continue down while the upper portion dries out.

3- A well-coated engobe piece must be at least 1/50 inch (0.5 mm) thick.

Dyed engobes

The importance of using dyed engobes lies in the possible color combinations that can be achieved. Because there are so many combinations, it is impossible to even exhaust them all, regardless of how experienced you are or how much you know.

Basic materials for dyeing

There are two types of materials used as colorants: metallic oxides and industrial dyes. Engobes themselves are used as fixatives for oxides and dyes, which means that oxides and dyes that have an engobe as part of their formula do not have any chance of running when they are in the kiln. On the other hand, pieces that do not have engobe as part of their mixture and are then covered with a layer of lead that is too thick have a greater chance of seeing their colors run or their glaze separate when they come out of the kiln. One inconvenience in working with engobes mixed with oxides is that the true colors are apparent only after the piece is baked. But this happens with every color produced chemically.

Different samples of dyes and oxides, mixed with engobe, after they have been baked and glazed.

Oxides

Oxides are natural materials. Most of them are metallic oxides and their range of colors is limited. In this raw state it is difficult to tell them apart, because their colors only range from blacks to grays. When they are fired, the colors change, depending on the type of glaze that is applied and the atmosphere in the kiln.

The most important oxides for beginning to work with ceramics are:

Chromium oxide (A), whose symbol is CrO, gives the engobe an opaque green color. It is applied between 1 and 5 percent. It is not recommended in higher proportions because it is a refractory material and can change the plasticity or refractivity of the engobe.

Copper oxide (B), whose symbol is CuO, changes completely when mixed with a glaze or an engobe. It is a difficult oxide to apply because it is sometimes volatile. It turns the color of green grass when mixed with an engobe. If you want to get a relatively stable color, it must be applied in a proportion of 3 to 5 percent. It can produce a metallic black color beyond 5 to 6 percent.

Cobalt oxide (C) is identified with the symbol CoO. It is the most intense oxide because it produces excellent blues in very small proportions. Amounts ranging from 0.250 to 1.5 percent can be added. Beyond 3 percent, it can produce dark blue tones or almost black.

Iron oxide (D), whose symbol is FeO, is perhaps the least spectacular mixed with an engobe. Its coloration ranges from light to dark brown. It generates colors of little interest outside the indicated proportions. It can be mixed from 3 to 8 percent. The best results are achieved with glazes.

Manganese dioxide (E), whose symbol is MnO$_2$, provides a brown pigmented color when mixed with an engobe, because the pigment is not very fine. It is interesting for certain types of decoration, and it can be mixed from 1 to 5 percent. Beyond 5 to 6 percent, the color begins to become metallic.

Tin oxide (F), whose chemical name is NiO, generates a semiopaque, grayish green color when mixed with an engobe. It can be used at 1 to 5 percent. It provides very interesting colors when mixed with these oxides.

Dyes

Dyes are industrial materials prepared mechanically with basic metal oxides and other materials. They exist for the purpose of complementing the range of colors of the oxides. The colors of the raw dyes are similar to those that result from firing, depending on the type of glaze that is applied over them. The proportion used for dyes is higher than for metallic oxides because the elements that have been added reduce the proportion of the color.

Color sample chart

Before the engobe mixture is prepared for decorating, make a color sample chart of the dyes. To do this, weigh out one of the previous formulas for single-fire engobes. For example, white clay, 2 ounces (60 g), kaolin 2/3 ounce (20 g), feldspar 1/3 ounce (10 g), and quartz 1/3 ounce (10 g). Add dyes in three different proportions, one of about 10 percent, a second of 20 percent, and another with 30 percent. Glaze and fire them. This way you will always have the samples as reference when you are ready to decorate.

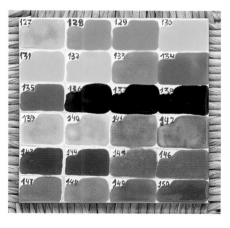

Sample chart with different proportions of dyes, fired and glazed.

Decorative techniques using engobes

Before you choose the decorative technique that you are going to use, you must know which glaze you are going to use to finish the piece. Although this subject will be covered later on, keep in mind that without some knowledge of glazes, it is difficult to get good results. Once you understand what the engobe is, its uses, its preparation, applications, and how to dye it, practice is a must.

Coffee set displaying several decorative techniques created with engobes.

Plate decorated with dyed engobe using a slip trailer, and then glazed. Work by Vila-Clara.

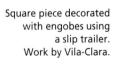

Square piece decorated with engobes using a slip trailer. Work by Vila-Clara.

Plate decorated with sgraffito, ready for glazing.

Preliminary instructions

When we talk about applying engobe, generally we are referring to the coating of the entire piece or part of it to change its color. However, once the color of the piece has been changed, there is still one more step: the decoration of the piece when the engobe has dried. This procedure is complicated and requires some attention at the beginning.

This chapter has emphasized the contraction between clays and engobes. So now, the dilemma of the contraction—a potter's primary concern—presents itself once again. This time between two engobes: the one used for dipping the piece and the other used for decorating.

In this case, contraction may occur because of some difference between the dry engobe and the wet engobe used for decoration. Sometimes this can cause certain problems, which must be corrected during the decorating process, if the application consists of simple color brushstrokes over the engobe. Normally, the brushstroke dries as soon as it is applied.

Caution with the thickness

Some traditional decorating techniques call for thick applications. This is used even to create relief. But some problems may arise at this point as a result of the contraction between dry and wet engobes. To avoid this problem, the density of the color must be monitored. If it is too thick, there will be more risk of cracking than if it were thinner. When you want to make very thick decorations with engobe, you must first apply several fine brushstrokes to wet the engobe on the piece, and then start adding layers gradually. If you apply engobe with a slip trailer or with any other tool that makes it difficult to control the thickness, you must correct the plasticity of the engobe's formula. This is done by adding between 5 and 10 percent quartz or feldspar to the mixture to make it more refractory.

Layering engobes

The decorative result obtained from pouring one or several engobes depends on the nature of the pieces, and in the color or contrast of the texture between the areas covered and exposed. The possibilities increase when one decoration overlaps the other, especially with colored engobes. If more than one color is used, the possibilities widen even more.

When the engobes are superimposed, the top layer is the dominant one, unless it is so thin that the bottom layer can be seen through it. A technical aspect to keep in mind in these cases is to make sure that the engobe has been stirred properly and that its consistency is maintained all the way through with the proper density. Another important technical aspect in both processes is not to create excessive thickness in the superimposed areas. Engobes that are too thick tend to flake off, unless they are perfectly bonded.

⌐1

1- First, apply a layer of a white or colored engobe to the bowl. Then trail some colored engobe with a slip trailer or with any other tool.

⌐2

2- Move the bowl slowly so the color can form decorative designs. Then, add a different color and repeat the movement slowly, until the desired effect is achieved.

Sgraffito

Sgraffito is the process of making lines on a layer of crude engobe to expose the surface that lies underneath. Upon entering the world of sgraffito, you are faced with two different aspects of this technique: fine linear design on the engobe and scratching a material to expose the one underneath. It is not necessary to cover either one in depth because the process of scratching is less difficult than most of the other ceramic procedures.

From the historical point of view, the most common application of sgraffito involves engobes. In many cultures where dark red baking clays are abundant, the only way to produce pieces lighter in color is by covering the red object with a white or colored engobe. In the pieces that receive this treatment, it is common to scratch through the engobe to expose the red clay, to get an immediate decoration.

The main characteristic of sgraffito is the contrast created between the scratched lines that leave the layer underneath exposed and the color of the engobe of the surface. It is important for the scratched surface not to loose its smooth quality, which is why the proper tool is necessary.

It is common for the borders of the designs to get ragged lines when they are traced on the soft engobe. If this is the case, the engobe should be allowed to dry completely, and then it can be cleaned with a brush.

The lines may vary dramatically, depending on the type of tool that is used or the degree of pressure applied. The lines that are made on the dry engobe tend to be delicate and irregular. To make sturdier lines that do not crack, the surface must be dampened with a sponge before the scratching process begins, or the sgraffito decoration must be made when the engobe is still damp.

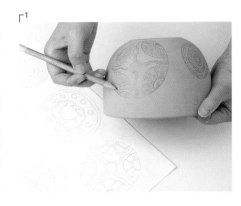

1- To begin the sgraffito, you must first outline the design to know how to decorate the piece. This design is later transferred to the piece by tracing it on with a pencil and applying light pressure.

2 and 3- Use a wooden tool to remove the portion of the engobe that you want to leave exposed.

4- Finished bowl with sgraffito, ready for bisque fire and glazing.

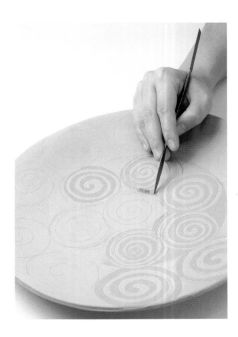

Any type of clay can be decorated with this technique. The background of the design will be the color of the clay chosen.

Decorating with a slip trailer

The technique that has become most popular in engobe decoration is, without a doubt, the traditional technique of slip trailing. Some of the most beautiful examples of old pottery are made using this technique and are well known worldwide. Also, some modern potters still use this technique in one way or another.

With some practice, engobe is relatively easy to apply, and it uses only one glaze, which is applied after the first firing. The most important aspect of this technique is to find the proper angle to hold the slip trailer, and the right consistency of the engobe to obtain the lightness and elegance that characterize the decorations made using this method.

Dots and lines are common visual elements in contemporary ceramic pieces decorated with engobe.

Detail of a design made with colored engobe, applied with a slip trailer.

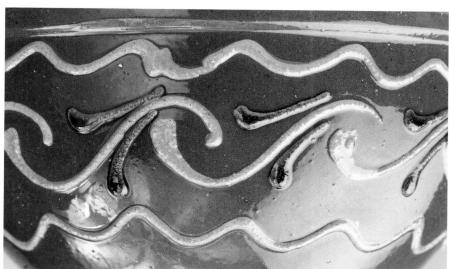

The application of blue, transparent glaze over the decorations made with colored engobe, helps to highlight the finish of the piece even more.

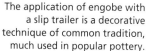

The application of engobe with a slip trailer is a decorative technique of common tradition, much used in popular pottery.

How to work with slip trailers

If you are going to decorate with a slip trailer, you must keep the consistency of the engobe in mind when preparing it, because it must be somewhat thicker than the one used for dipping.

When working with this technique, remember for both aesthetic and technical reasons that you are dealing with a liquid material. Therefore, only if you work nonstop and have a good, flexible rubber slip trailer will you achieve the desired quality.

It is very important to have a good slip trailer made with flexible rubber so it can be fitted with several spouts of different sizes. It must be easy to clean, and easy and fast to fill up.

To fill up the slip trailer, first press on it to remove all the air. Then, insert it in the container, and release the grip slowly to begin filling it up.

A

B

C

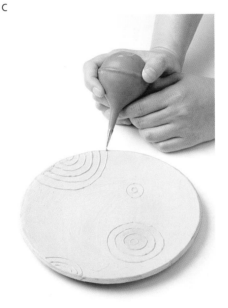

Slip trailer decorations can be made on a damp base that has recently been covered with engobe (A), on a leather hard base that has no engobe (B), or on a base with engobe that has dried leather hard (C).

A different engobe has been applied over the already-dried engobe of these two pieces. In these cases, the dry base has a less fluid quality than a base that has no engobe and is damp, but it provides limitless possibilities for relief. Independently of its thickness, not having a damp base provides the opportunity for more deliberate work.

Decorating with dots and lines

The visual elements of this technique consist of long lines and dots or small marks. The lines can be long or short, depending on the pressure applied on the rubber slip trailer or on the speed of the hand. The dots can also be different sizes. However, both elements are the main configurations of this technique. The rubber slip trailers used for this type of decoration must be kept full all the time. They work better if they are filled up before the procedure begins and held perfectly upright.

1- Apply pressure on the slip trailer to remove all the air, until the engobe begins to drip out.

2- Place the slip trailer face down. Pressure keeps the engobe from coming out of the tip of the spout.

3- Before starting, it is a good idea to practice on a clean cardboard scrap to loosen up. Light pressure is applied at the beginning of the process until the engobe starts to come out.

4- Slight pressure is sufficient to maintain a steady flow of engobe, and reducing the pressure will stop it.

Another example of decoration with dots and lines made with colored engobe, and applied with a slip trailer.

Working with a rubber slip trailer that is almost empty, or with more or less air pressure inside, is to tempt fate, because each time the engobe comes out and air goes in, a miniature explosion occurs. The unavoidable result is a glob of engobe on the surface of the piece.

Burnishing

The burnishing technique is very old, and it is still widely practiced in many traditional cultures. The clays used in the old days were formed with fine particles, because they were sifted over and over. These clays had high melting points, which made them susceptible to rudimentary baking, and the burnished surface had more intensity and sheen. However, keep in mind that pieces were burnished to make them waterproof—that is, to close the pores of the surface so the objects could be used as domestic utensils.

The burnishing technique

The burnishing technique involves rubbing the leather-hard clay continuously and persistently. Its goal is to give the clay a smooth finish and to achieve a sheen that is good enough to make glazing unnecessary.

Burnishing is an easy procedure. One simply needs to find a flat tool and to rub it firmly against the clay. It can be a smooth river pebble, the back of a spoon, a wooden stick, a throwing rib, or even your fingernails. As long as it is made of a hard and smooth material, it does not make any difference which one it is. The only thing to keep in mind is that the shape of the tool should allow the surface to be worked easily. All types of clay can be burnished more or less intensely, but nowadays it is difficult to find the clays that were in use when this technique originated. Besides, the goal today is generally to make artistic pieces.

Burnishing must be done when the clay is leather hard. If the surface is too soft, the tool will leave marks, and it will be very difficult to make it smooth. Nowadays there are two times when common clays can loose their sheen after burnishing. First, while the piece is drying out, in which case it can be burnished again when it is almost dry. And second, during firing, which means that the temperature is too high or that the clay is not sufficiently pure. The problem can be corrected in two ways: by adding engobe to the piece and working it when it becomes leather hard, which will allow you to work with any color, producing much better results, or reducing the firing temperature. The approximate temperature to maintain the gloss of the burnished pieces ranges between 1,652°F and 1,730°F (900°C and 950°C).

To ensure that a burnished piece made with modern clays does not lose its sheen during baking, a rudimentary firing method should be used, such as a wood stove. This firing is done at a very low temperature, and the uncontrolled shrinkage that occurs helps close the clay's pores that have been previously covered with a fine tool.

1 and 2- When the piece is leather hard, the engobe is added to provide the color. Two or three colors can be used to make the object more decorative.

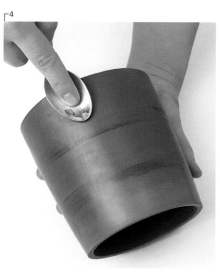

3- After the piece has been painted, remove any ragged edges that may have appeared with a throwing rib.

4- Burnish the piece by rubbing it with a teaspoon.

5- The process that is required to leave the surface completely smooth is slow and labor intensive. Inspect the piece with a hand, to ensure that all spots have been burnished.

6 and 7- When the piece is completely burnished, it can be decorated with good sgraffito, leaving some areas burnished, and some scratched.

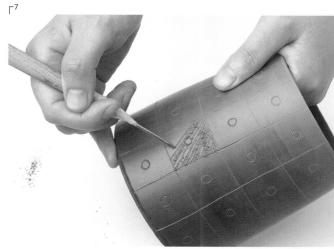

8- You can burnish all kinds of pieces, whether made on the potter's wheel or formed by hand or with molds.

9- Piece finished ready to be baked.

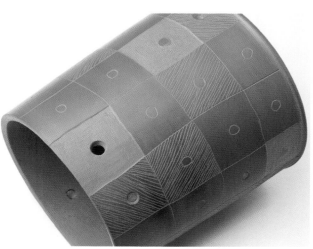

Resist

Using resist, an artist can control the decorative process. Covering some areas of the object protects them against application of decorative material. The resist prevents the engobe from reaching the clay base, and some parts of the piece remain undecorated, eliminating the need for scratching or cleaning. Aside from these two simple applications, it is also possibile to cover areas or outline designs using different techniques.

Various materials can be used on the engobe to act as a resist, such as wax, strips of newspaper, latex, or a pattern.

Making resist patterns with newspaper

Newspaper resist patterns are used on leather-hard clays before the engobe is applied. Technically, there are two very important factors: the quality of the paper and its dampness. The newspaper piece adapts perfectly to the shape of the object when it is wetted, and it does not present any difficulty.

The success of the newspaper medium depends basically on the care with which it is applied over the clay. Independently from the degree of moisture, it must stay perfectly adhered to the object, which will have been previously dampened with a sponge. When all pieces have been properly arranged, they will be wiped again with the damp sponge to eliminate any excess water from the surface.

The engobe must be applied as soon as the paper is positioned correctly. It is advisable to avoid making brusque movements that will cause the edges of the paper to become detached. The techniques for applying the engobes are the same as the ones explained earlier in this same chapter.

1- Cut a few pieces of paper, and wet them with a sprayer or a sponge.

2- Place the pieces of paper on the object, making sure that they adhere to the surface properly and do not form air bubbles.

3- Apply the engobe to the piece with a brush, or by dipping the object in it, whichever you consider more appropriate.

4- When the engobe is leather hard, 3 to 4 hours after the application, lift off the newspaper pieces.

5- The finished piece ready for firing.

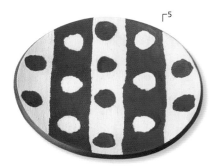

Making a resist with any paper

Resist is a very interesting decorative technique that allows the use of any type of paper. The possibilities are endless.

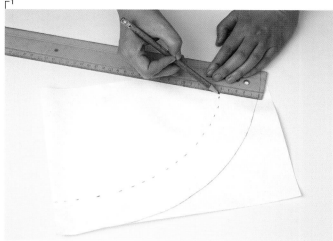

1- You can use any paper that you have handy—for example a regular sheet of writing paper. In this case, the shape of the object must first be drawn on the piece of paper.

2- Lay the paper over the piece to cut it to size.

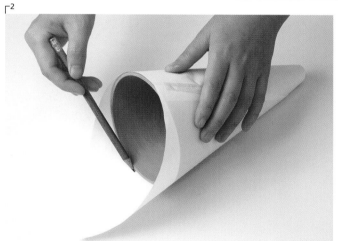

3 and 4- After the paper has been cut, glue it to the piece, and begin to draw.

5- After the design has been drawn, cut out some parts of it, and use them to make a resist and to complete the decoration.

6- Paint the entire piece with a different colored engobe.

7- After a period of time, between 15 and 30 minutes, remove the paper.

8- Go over the outline with a tool to clean up any edges that have smeared.

9- Continue with the decoration of the piece using the sgraffito technique.

10- Then, proceed to decorate the inside of the object.

11- When the decoration with the resist is finished, you can continue making creative motifs with oxides or dyes.

12- View of the finished piece before firing.

Decorating with brushes

Decorating with brushes is the technique that offers the widest range of possibilities in ceramics. It is done using a colored engobe, which is applied to unbaked clay at the point when the piece is leather hard or completely dry. The color, the piece, and the moment it is decorated—together with the personal touch of the artist—are the factors that contribute to the personality of the piece.

Painting is a process that requires artistic skill, and the novice confronted with this technique for the first time can rarely escape that fact.

Once you have tried out the materials and brushes you want to use, there is still a long road ahead for tests and experimentation. After all, repetition can help you let loose your imagination and enable you to create without limitations.

The brushes

The condition of the brushes, the timing of the application, and the type of material to be applied are all factors to keep in mind.

The brush's bristles must retain a certain amount of the liquid and release it continuously, to even the surface out as it moves along. When the brush is charged with engobe, its tip is rounded, and it becomes more elongated as the paint passes to the surface.

It is difficult to recommend which type of brush is best for decorating because in the field of ceramics there is a series of materials that can be applied, with different consistencies and weights, and the brushes that would work for one type would not work for the other.

Many factors influence the quality of the painted decoration. Understanding the effect that the thickness of the material will create on the body chosen

is one of them, and the content, placement, and color are others. But the main factor is the pressure applied on the brush that is being used.

The brushes do not simply make marks: They express the direction of the stroke. However, marks that are made too fast can look uneven. If this could be prevented, the marks would look more fluid.

The factors that can help you achieve this fluidity are the clarity of your intention and a good dose of experience using the brushes and the materials for each decorative context.

You can acquire both by practicing on paper. The work done on a piece of paper helps define the ideas, which is why you should make it a habit of starting each project with a sketch.

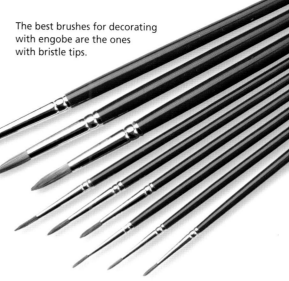

The best brushes for decorating with engobe are the ones with bristle tips.

⌐2

⌐1

1- Normally you begin painting a piece after it has been covered with engobe.

2- Before you begin to decorate a piece, you must have an idea of how many designs you want to apply. In the technique of engobes, sgraffito is usually applied after painting, to give more volume to the decoration.

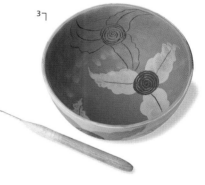
3⌐

4⌐

3 and 4- Inside and outside view of the finished bowl ready for glazing and firing.

1 and 2- More ideas on how to use engobe to decorate objects that can be finished with other techniques.

1 and 2- In other cases, after painting you can touch up with a slip trailer to add volume to some areas.

Spiral lines provide richness and freedom of expression, which is very appropriate for the inside of a bowl.

Intarsia

This technique in ceramics cannot be compared to its great tradition in other media. In the world of ceramics, examples of great quality can be found in the traditions of other cultures, and in the beginnings of decoration during the seventeenth century, an era in which this technique was prevalent.

The basic requirement for using this technique is to have a good pattern. If you cannot find one in specialized stores, make one yourself using tracing paper that is waterproof and can be reused.

The easiest technique for working with intarsia is to use a single cutout design and a pattern. Aside from the difficulty of the project, it's important to determine whether it requires different colors or several patterns, their placement, and the density of the engobe. The engobe to be applied must be very thick, so much that the brush should be able to stay upright inside the container. Any thinner and it can seep under the edges of the pattern and cause smearing.

1- First, make a simple sketch.

2- Place the pattern on the piece and paint over it. The engobe can be applied with any brush. The first coat is applied by brushing from one of the edges toward the center, and the second, from the other edge to the center. This way there is consistency in the intensity of the paint.

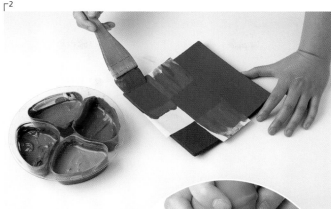

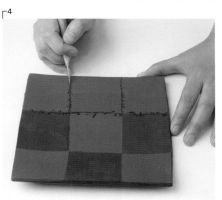

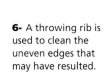

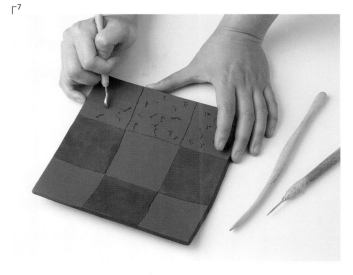

3- The pattern should be lifted carefully to prevent the wet paint from smearing.

4- Then, apply the other decorations to finish the piece. In this case, sgraffito is used to define the squares.

5- The next step will consist of a few details with the slip trailer to add some relief to the piece.

6- A throwing rib is used to clean the uneven edges that may have resulted.

7- Sgraffito is applied to the rest of the piece.

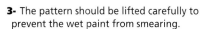

8- The details should be reviewed one last time.

9- This is how it will look before it goes in the kiln.

Glazing and underglazing

Underglazing decoration (done with pure oxides and dyes) and glazing give the objects an appearance that defines them as pottery pieces. The application of glaze to a piece and its subsequent baking is one of the most delicate phases of the pottery production. From this point on, any mistakes that may occur are impossible to correct. The glaze turns into a glassy layer that covers the pieces, making their surfaces smooth and waterproof. Vitrification is achieved from the effects of the heat in the oven. The use of transparent, low-firing glazes are ideal, because they really let the decoration show through.

Underglazed decoration

In general, underglazed decoration refers to all the decorative designs applied to the piece before it is waterproofed with glazing. However, the pottery world reserves this term for decoration done with pure oxides and dyes mixed with water, which is added when the piece is bisque. This type of decoration can be applied whether the piece has been covered with engobe or not.

Oxides and dyes

As we have already learned in the section dedicated to engobe, oxides are natural basic materials with a limited color range. Dyes, on the other hand, are industrial raw materials prepared by machine using metallic oxides and other products. Their range of colors is more varied, and complements those of oxides.

In underglazed decoration, both oxides and dyes are dissolved in water. When mixing them, it is important to keep in mind that the resulting product must have a liquid consistency—otherwise you could have problems with the glaze separating. Also, it is important that 20 percent of a very low temperature frit (see *Glazing*) must be added to dyes. For example, a frit of 1,112°F (600°C) would be fine.

Decorating a piece with commercial dyes mixed with water.

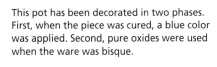

This pot has been decorated in two phases. First, when the piece was cured, a blue color was applied. Second, pure oxides were used when the ware was bisque.

Decorating with brushes

The freest form of expression in a decorative process is working with a brush, which obeys the movements of the hand, and always acts according to our wishes.

The application process is so simple, yet at the same time so complex, that it is difficult to arrive at a specific expla-

nation. The only solution for controlling this process is to practice, and to keep practicing until the technique has been fully mastered.

It is a good idea to make a sample chart previous to decorating. This will help you know which color to use, and what thickness must be applied, as well as which type of glaze is appropriate for the final layer.

Color samples done with a brush, before decorating the piece permanently.

1- Mark the design of your choice on the surface of the piece, using a pencil.

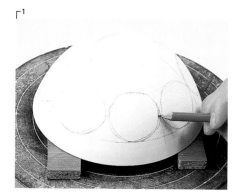

2- Prepare the color with a spatula, forming a paste completely dissolved in water.

3- With the piece resting on a slab base, circular lines are drawn by holding the brush stationary at one point.

4- The rest of the decoration is done while holding the piece in your hand.

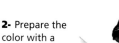

5- The inside of the piece had been decorated with a spiral, to which other patterns of a different color have been added.

6- Two views of the piece completely decorated.

1- In this example, the decoration is applied without drawing it with a pencil beforehand.

2- First, the color, which will have a very watery consistency, is applied, and then the outlines are painted using a color of a thicker consistency.

3- The application of a very diluted paint provides different nuances of the same color to the decoration.

4 and 5- To give the figures more definition and depth, their details can be outlined with a thicker brushstroke of the same color.

6- Finished pieces decorated with freehand brushstrokes, done without a preliminary drawing.

Resist

Decorating with resist is a common practice among potters, and it can be done whether a piece has been fired or not.

This technique is commonly used for two reasons during the glazing stage: One is to prevent the glaze from running onto the base of certain pieces, and second, to create a clean separation when the inside and outside of an object have been glazed with different materials.

Aside from these simple and formal applications, resist is also used to mark off areas and designs to work sgraffito on them.

Different materials can be used to work on the resist—for example, wax, latex, or contact paper.

Pieces decorated with hot wax-resist. The motifs have been drawn with a brush.

Cold wax has been used on this bowl to mask the surface. It has been decorated with iron oxide diluted in water.

Using wax

Cold and hot waxes can be used as a resist. Cold wax is a prepared emulsion that can be purchased in any specialty store. Hot wax is a mixture of wax paste diluted with essence of turpentine and warmed up in a double boiler.

To remove the wax from the surface of the piece, it must be bisque fired.

Both types of wax can be used without any problem, but each one of them has its pros and cons.

• Cold wax

This wax can be purchased ready to use, but it presents a small inconvenience. It takes a long time to dry, and if the layer is very thin, it is not sufficiently resistant to some types of water solutions. It is, however, very easy and fast to work with.

• Hot wax

This wax dries immediately after it has been spread, and even if the layer is very thin, it resists any type of liquid.

Despite the difficulty of its preparation, hot wax makes a superior product if it is well prepared and used at the appropriate temperature.

To achieve a good temperature level, the traditional method can be used, inserting the can with the wax into a double boiler (putting it inside another that contains boiling water to keep the wax in a liquid state so it can be applied easily over the piece).

Brushes used for applying wax should be reserved exclusively for this purpose. The brush should never be left inside the hot wax, not even for a few minutes, because it will completely lose its shape.

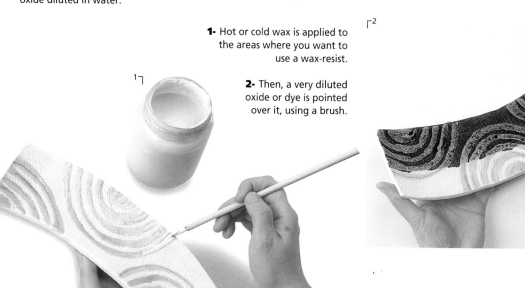

1- Hot or cold wax is applied to the areas where you want to use a wax-resist.

2- Then, a very diluted oxide or dye is pointed over it, using a brush.

⌐3

3- The areas covered with wax are not colored. When the piece is bisque fired, the wax that has not been removed will melt in the oven.

4⌐

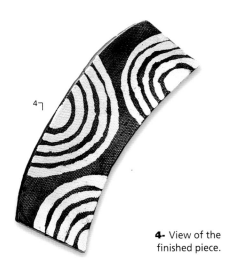

4- View of the finished piece.

Using latex

Latex is an emulsion that can be purchased ready to use in specialty stores.

Prepared latex almost always has to have water added to thin it, so it can be applied easily.

However, take care not to dilute the mixture too much, because the film would be too thin, and it would break when being removed.

Latex can be applied to any type of piece or a resist made with it on any surface. Although the latex is a substance that dissolves in water, it has a tendency to ruin the brushes. If the latex turns rubbery on the brush, or if you're working with it for more than 15 minutes, it is advisable to wash the brush well with tap water before continuing.

Latex can be used for decorating with engobe, or be applied to baked clays before they are glazed. It is advisable to make several tests before its final application, to be able to control its thickness, how it dissolves, and drying.

1- The latex is applied over the surface with a brush. As soon as it loses its milky appearance and the surface has acquired a matte texture, the decoration process begins.

⌐1

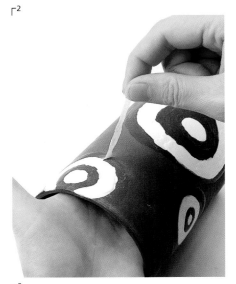

⌐2

⌐3

2 and 3- When the dye has been applied with a brush and it is completely dry, the corner of the latex can be lifted and pulled, beginning at this point, to remove it. This will expose the areas previously covered with the resist.

⌐
4

4- Then, the glaze of your choice can be applied and the piece fired.

Using contact paper patterns

This process is most commonly done on bisqueware. The use of this technique, which offers a good number of possibilities when creating well-defined areas, is considered a technological advance of the twentieth century. The reason for this is that for the patterns to remain well bonded, the process must be done on a computer, especially if letters are used. Then, the patterns are cut out with a plotter. If you do not have a plotter, but you have a computer, you can save the design on a disk, and contact a company that makes signs. These companies have cutting plotters, and they can cut out the design for a (usually) reasonable price, returning it to you on contact paper ready to stick on.

1- Place the contact paper on the surface of the piece, and use a knife to remove the areas that you wish to decorate.

2- Paint with any oxide or dye, using a brush. The areas covered with the contact paper will resist the paint.

3 and 4- When the object has been painted, remove the contact paper, and the piece is ready for glazing and baking.

5 and 6- Finished negative and positive pieces. In this case, they have been treated with a glossy, transparent glaze.

Decorating with a sponge

The decorations made with a sponge are very simple and easy to apply. They are generally used to complement other decorations, or as the background color of a piece. Stamping is one form of this technique.

2- Choose a sponge piece and wet it with dye.

3- Place the sponge on the surface of the object applying light pressure.

4- Choose another piece of sponge, wet it with a different dye, and apply it on the object with the help of a wooden stick.

5- You can finish decorating the piece with a brush.

1- Take a few pieces of sponge and shape them according to your needs.

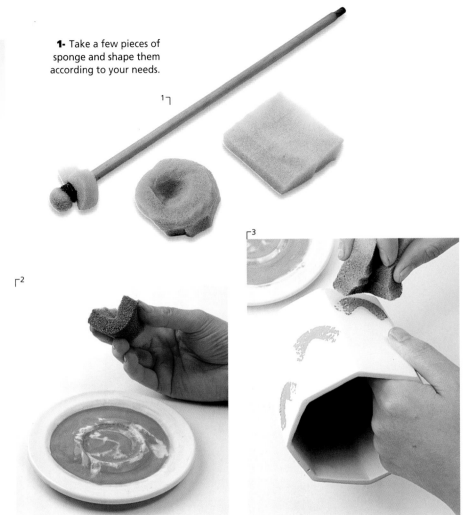

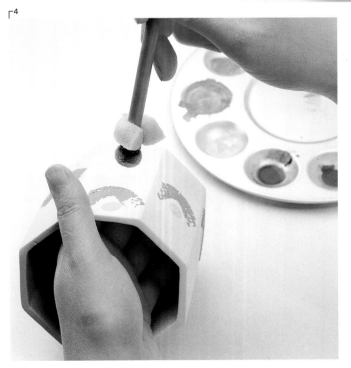

Choose the chalk that you want to work with.

Decorating with colored chalk or crayons

You can use a number of materials for underglazed decoration—for example, colored chalk or crayons. These pigments are made with metallic oxides or with industrial dyes.

It is easy to make your own chalk or crayons. You will need white clay, to which oxide or dye will be added gradually. For oxides you add between 1 percent and 5 percent, and between 10 percent and 30 percent for dyes, depending on the color intensity desired. When everything is mixed thoroughly, and after making sure that the colored clay is even all the way through, a long band of the desired thickness is formed. You can also place some of the colored clay in a slip trailer to make relief decorations. When the chalk has been finished, it is put aside to dry out completely, and then it is fired at a temperature between 1,292°F and 1,472°F (700°C and 800°C). This is sufficient temperature to harden it so it can be used for marking. Specialized stores sell colored crayons that have been prepared using the same process, and they can be used like colored pencils.

1- Draw the design that you want on the piece with a pencil.

You can also use colored pencils.

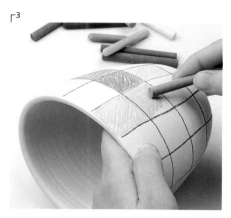

2- The upper part of the piece, which is made with black clay, is decorated with white chalk.

1- In this example, we draw a sketch of the design using a colored pencil.

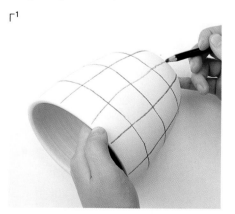

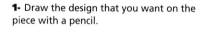

2 and 3- The squares are filled in with different colors.

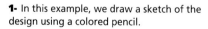

Glazing

Glazing is the last phase before the piece is fired, and is a crucial moment in the creative process. Any mistake is very hard to correct once you've reached this point.

The main goal of glazing is forming a glass-like coating that covers the pottery, to make the object waterproof. Sometimes, the purpose is simply to decorate it. These glazes are normally transparent, and can either have color or not. They can also be either glossy or matte.

The finish

In ceramics, there are several possible finishes that can be used on the surface of any object coated, glazed, vitrified, or enameled. They all have the same purpose, which is to form a glass-like film that will cover the surface of the piece.

However, the first three terms refer to a transparent coating, whether glossy or matte. The fourth is understood to be an opaque layer, which can also be glossy or matte.

Ceramic composition decorated with engobe using a slip trailer, and covered with a layer of yellow transparent glaze. Work by J. Vila Clara.

The inside of this bowl has been preserved with a transparent blue glaze. For the outside, on the other hand, a transparent and colorless glaze has been used.

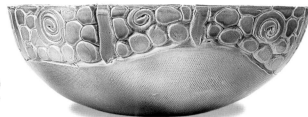

Vase decorated with a very watery oxide, and covered with a transparent matte glaze. Work by D. Fita.

Container covered with a blue transparent glaze.

Bowl decorated with engobe and covered with a colorless, transparent glaze.

So, the finish can be transparent glossy or matte depending on the amount that is used, and the ingredients, and the amounts of each in the composition. This will give the pieces a range of different colors.

The transparent, glossy, or matte finishes are the ones through which the surface of the clay can be seen, and therefore the decoration that is underneath. When referring to the three aforementioned finishes that can be applied to clay, coated, glazed, and vitrified, we will use the term *glaze* because it is the one that adapts best to the characteristics of the creative process explained here.

The glossy and matte opaque finishes are the ones that do not allow us to see through to the clay of the body. Therefore, it is obvious that they block the view of any decoration that it may have.

The surface of this piece has been made waterproof with a colorless and matte transparent glaze. Work by D. Fita.

These two pieces have been made waterproof with an opaque coating that hides the color of the clay.

Composition and types of glazes

Chemically, a glaze is composed of mineral salts formed by reactions between acids and bases. The basic component in its elaboration is silica (SiO_2), which alone would be enough to form a glaze. However, its use is limited due to its high fusion point of 3,100°F (1,730°C). This is why compounds with a lower melting point are added—to lower the fusion point of the silica.

Therefore, the basic materials that form the glaze can be classified in two groups: The first corresponds to the basic materials that melt easily, like lead, borax, sodium, potash, lithium, and calcium; the second comprises those with high melting points, like quartz, alumina, and magnesium.

There are also two kinds of glazes—ash and frit—depending on whether they have been previously baked or not. The first category includes glazes that have been made from natural minerals, which can be weighed in order to vary proportion according to the characteristics that you wish to give the glaze.

The second category includes the group of basic materials that are used to form a glaze that has been previously baked. They can be defined as a mixture of different materials that, through a fusion process, go from a solid state to a liquid state, and in subsequent cooling form a vitreous mass that must be ground and pulverized. Mixing this powder with water, a liquid is obtained that can be applied to the surface of pottery pieces.

Group of vases with blue glaze. Work by J. Marcet and R. Vila Abadal.

Piece glazed with a colorless frit. Work by J. Vila Clara.

Boxes covered with a colorless, transparent glaze. Work by J. Marcet and R. Vila Abadal.

Frit glazes

To know the exact amount of raw material that must be added to make a frit base, you must make a calculation. This calculation, as well as the formula for making these glazes, is a complex and specialized process, because it is not a skill that can be acquired simply by chance. Therefore, we will not cover in this book the formulation of the glazes—we will only refer to those that can be found in any store that sells pottery supplies.

These glazes are sold in small quantities, already prepared to be mixed with water. It is a good idea for beginners in this field to use these prepared glazes first, which are usually of excellent quality. When they have acquired some experience in their use and methods of handling, they can begin to experiment with mixtures made from many of the formulas found in basic ceramics books, or based on what they have learned in a class for this artistic activity.

The purpose of the frit

This process eliminates part of the toxic components in products such as lead.

It also suppresses solubility of the substances that have this quality, and therefore the result is a product that is not soluble in water. Such is the case with boric acid.

With it, one also has certain confidence about the consistency of glazes, and the same color and texture are obtained every time.

This procedure is seldom used by artist potters, because a difference in color is a desired quality in the finishing process of certain pieces. On the other hand, it is a vital method for mass production.

A drop of frit inside a bowl decorated with relief.
Work by Yukiko Murata.

Making a frit

First, the components for the frit are weighed and mixed dry. Then, the weighed materials are placed in the crucible of a frit kiln, filling it up only halfway, and closing the oven afterwards. There is a moment when the frit reaches appropriate fluidity, and the products change from a solid to a liquid state. At this point, the liquid begins to drip out of a hole. It is very important to place a container filled with cold water beneath the hole where the glaze comes out, so the frit will slowly drip into it when the process of fusion begins. With the sudden cooling, the glaze shatters into small, very brittle particles, which can be easily ground in a ball mill.

When the frit is finished, it must be ground in the ball mill until the desired grain consistency is achieved. After grinding, the product is dried to separate the ground product from the water. For best results, the product is usually placed in a dryer or inside the oven at a temperature between 122°F and 212°F (50°C and 100°C). When the frit is dry, it is weighed, and after checking the weight, other products are added. When this process is finished, the glazes are ready to use.

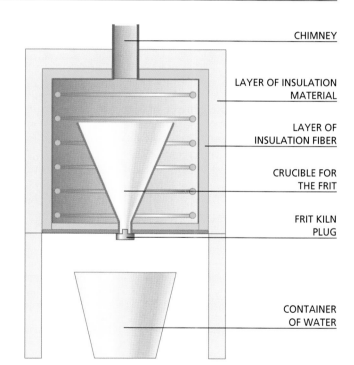

CHIMNEY

LAYER OF INSULATION MATERIAL

LAYER OF INSULATION FIBER

CRUCIBLE FOR THE FRIT

FRIT KILN PLUG

CONTAINER OF WATER

Diagram of how a kiln works to make the frit.

Ball mill for grinding the frit. When the cylinder rotates, the soapstone balls that are inside pulverize the frit.

Classifying frit glazes

To be able to handle frit glazes more easily, we will classify them so you can understand them better and be able to choose the type of glaze depending on your color palette.

They can be classified in three large groups according to their qualities and characteristics. The first group comprises lead glazes, the second boron, and the third alkaline glazes.

To select the coating that best meets your needs, you can make a sample chart of the different frit glazes you have to choose from.

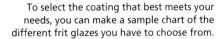

• Lead frits or glazes
First of all, it must be pointed out that lead has a big drawback: **it is toxic.** If the lead dust is absorbed through the skin or the respiratory or digestive systems, it is difficult to eliminate, and can cause serious intoxication. All types and qualities of lead frits can be found in specialized pottery stores. You should test these glazes and experiment with them beforehand. Also, when you buy them, you must be careful and check if they conform to the legal requirements on toxicity levels.

Another problem is that lead dissolves when attacked by an acid. Lead and quartz frits reduce this problem somewhat.

However, this is the most efficient and most used flux in low and medium-fire glaze. That is, the piece can be fired between approximately 1,472°F and 2,012°F (800°C and 1,100°C).

Through history and in many modern cultures, we have found examples of this type of glaze. The advantages of using lead are obvious—it combines easily with most the other materials, and produces glazes of great luminosity. It has an important characteristic that must be remembered, and that helps set it apart—it provides yellowish tones in its results, and the range includes warm and attractive color tones. Besides, although its texture is very transparent, and glossy, it is very easy to make opaque and matte glazes with it.

Glazed piece with a glossy, transparent lead frit.

Bright and glossy colors can be created with a lead frit.

• Alkaline frits or glazes

Alkaline glazes are those with bases consisting mainly of potassium, sodium, and lithium alkaline oxides. Alkaline glazes also have an important drawback—they are not very hard, and tend to crack considerably. This means that if they are applied on a porous body, the water resistance of the piece is compromised. As a contrast, the best-known property of alkaline glazes is precisely the enormous influence that they have over metallic glazes. Together with them, they create very clear and pure tones. So, turquoise colors are excellent parting from alkaline oxides with copper oxide (CuO). They are also ideal for making crackle glazes.

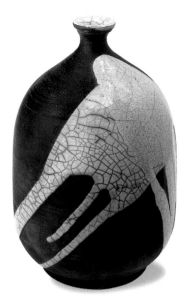

Vase colored with copper oxide and glazed with an alkaline frit. The combination of copper oxide and an alkaline glaze results in a turquoise color. Notice also, the crackle effect achieved due to the use of an alkaline glaze.

• Boron frits or glazes

In general, boron is added to a glaze because of its qualities as a flux and its ability to work at very low temperatures. Boron is an excellent product, because it is possible to make glazes from a temperature of 1,382°F (750°C) and up. In addition to being a good flux, boron also offers the advantage of forming elastic glazes with a low surface tension, preventing cracking. This is the reason why boron glazes are preferable to alkaline glazes. At the same time, they have similar properties, like the tendency to form turquoise colors with copper oxide (CuO).

Boron must not be applied in large quantities, because it promotes the melting process and can form bubbles and drip on the kiln's bat.

In the form of boric acid, barium is very soluble in water, and due to this technical characteristic it must be used as a frit. This does not mean that it can't be used raw in small quantities and mixed with other products, but there is always an element of mystery which could upset the results.

This piece has been covered with a colorless, alkaline glaze, in contrast with the one that appears on the previous page that is glazed with a glossy, transparent lead frit. The result is whiter tonality and less gloss.

Group of pieces waterproofed with transparent, matte, colorless glaze. Work by J. Marcet and R. Vila Abadal.

Plate glazed with a glossy, transparent, and colorless boron frit.

Raw materials for dyeing glazes

The same compounds that are used to dye clays or engobe can also be used to dye glazes.

Until now, we have only dealt with the basic principles for the elaboration of colorless glazes. There are two large groups of materials that we have mentioned previously that are used for coloring glazes—metallic oxides and industrial dyes.

Oxides

Although there are relatively few oxides available, it is possible to make an ample range of colors with them, and there are many factors that influence their dyeing effect. The primary one is the chemical composition of the glaze. Other factors are temperature, the atmosphere of the kiln, the color of the clay, the thickness of the glaze, and so on.

Because raw metallic oxide has a very different color from one that has been fired, one must be aware of its effects before using it.

Several of the oxides have different qualities depending on the materials they are combined with.

They must be applied with a very liquid consistency—otherwise, they can easily turn to a metallic black and smear.

Dyes

Industrial dyes are other materials that can influence the color and the appearance of the glaze. These dyes have very different characteristics than those of the oxides. They can be mixed with the glaze to provide color, but they tend to turn opaque. If you want to create transparent glazes with them, they must be applied in very small quantities.

The commercial or prepared dyes are easier and more reliable than the oxides. It is possible to make out its color when it is raw, but as with oxides, its tonality varies considerably depending on the type of glaze that it is mixed with: lead, boron, or alkaline glaze.

Samples of oxides in pure form.

Piece made using the sgraffito technique, and covered with a yellow glaze with an iron oxide base. Work by D. Fita and D. Ros.

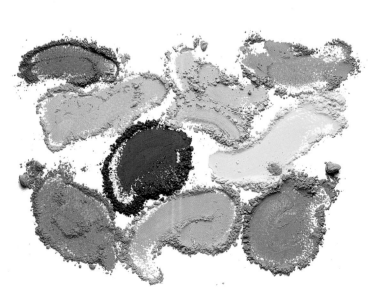

Samples of commercial dyes.

Applying glazes

The final result of the pieces that you make will depend greatly on the application of the glazes.

Before the glaze is applied, remember to clean the piece carefully, removing any dust, either with a wet sponge or a dry cloth. Next, the glaze should be stirred repeatedly and left in suspension.

The application method (brush, dipping, or spraying with a spray gun) should be decided in advance.

Using a brush

After the brush has been submerged in the glaze, it must be stirred vigorously. If the solution becomes suspended too fast, it must be stirred each time before the brush touches the piece. To prevent the glaze from settling too quickly, 2 percent Epsom salts (magnesium sulfate) or magnesium carbonate may be added.

To achieve a good glazing coat with the brush, the brush containing the liquid glaze must not be dragged on the piece, but instead leaned on it. To do this, an area of the piece is chosen, on which the brush will be placed the first time, and then the color is applied continuously from that initial point. The movement of your hand that applies the color must be rhythmic. The pressure will be constant. The brush is used as if it were a needle, that is, trying to maintain it upright, without bending the hair. Sometimes, the clay where the brush is placed can be too absorbent. In such cases, a little bit of water must be added to the glaze to ease application.

1- When the glaze is applied to the surface of the piece, the brush should not be charged, but wiped softly and superficially.

2- The entire surface should be covered with a thin layer of the glaze.

These pictures illustrate two different moments in the glazing process of a piece using a brush.

Using a spray gun

To apply the glaze in spray form you must have a spray gun—if possible, one with a reservoir on top. In addition to the gun, an air compressor is required, which should not be too big. The first tool sprays the material onto the piece, while the second provides the compressed air that makes the spray gun work. The application of glaze by spraying with a gun is much easier than application with a brush. The only difficulty is that practice is needed in use of the gun. This procedure allows the glaze to be spread smoothly and evenly. It also makes it possible to produce very delicate blending effects in any color, and to superimpose colors so exactly, that the effects and results achieved in the kiln are extraordinary.

When the glaze is applied with the gun, you must keep certain precautionary measures in mind. First, it is essential to use a face mask to avoid inhaling the spray, because it usually has toxic components. Second, the work must be done in an area with good ventilation

Compressor that provides pressurized air, which the gun needs to spray the pulverized glaze.

equipment that can remove the particles. And finally, the gun must be cleaned thoroughly after each use. It is best to take it apart, clean it with a rag wetted with oil, and to store it disassembled until the next use.

Spray gun for glazing. Its use allows the glaze to be spread evenly on the surface.

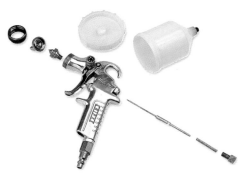

Spray gun for glazing, disassembled. It is best to take it apart and to clean it thoroughly after each use.

Using a bath or dipping

Another method of spreading the layer of glaze evenly is with a bath (or dipping). To use this method, you must have enough glaze to be able to submerge the pieces. This is perhaps the only drawback of this process, because it is not always practical to have such large quantities of glaze.

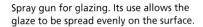
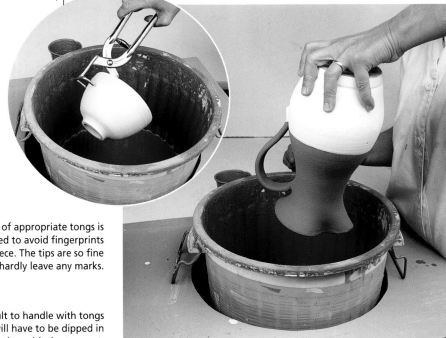

1- The use of appropriate tongs is recommended to avoid fingerprints on the piece. The tips are so fine that they hardly leave any marks.

2- If the piece is difficult to handle with tongs because of its size, it will have to be dipped in two stages, beginning with the top part.

3- For hollow pieces whose interior and exterior must be glazed, the operation begins with the inside.

4- The glaze is poured inside the piece, and after rotating it to make sure that the inside surface is covered, the glaze is poured out.

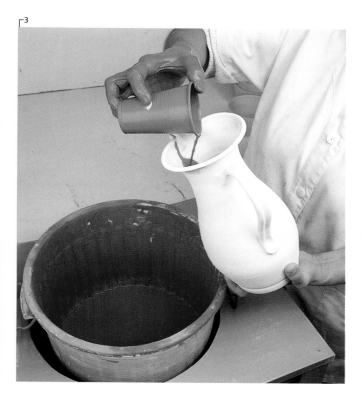

5- When the top part of the outside surface is dry, the bottom is dipped. Some glossy glazes adhere so well that the difference of the dipping stages is hardly noticeable. But if the glaze is matte, care should be taken when dipping it in two stages.

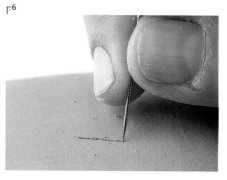

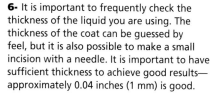

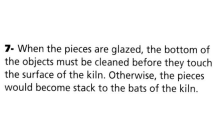

6- It is important to frequently check the thickness of the liquid you are using. The thickness of the coat can be guessed by feel, but it is also possible to make a small incision with a needle. It is important to have sufficient thickness to achieve good results—approximately 0.04 inches (1 mm) is good.

7- When the pieces are glazed, the bottom of the objects must be cleaned before they touch the surface of the kiln. Otherwise, the pieces would become stack to the bats of the kiln.

8- The excess glaze on the base of the objects can be cleaned easily using a wet sponge. When the pieces have been glazed and are ready for firing, it is necessary to place them in the kiln as soon as possible to keep particles of dust or other impurities from settling on them.

6 Firing

The last and most important phase in
creating a pottery piece is firing it. As the
culmination of a long and involved creative process,
firing can provide unimaginable pleasure—or, if an error
has been made, great frustration.
In firing, the kiln plays an important role—it is a vital tool.
Temperature is also critical, and that's why this chapter is devoted
to the main types of kilns and their applications and to the different
phases of firing. It is important to follow the advice exactly,
because the final quality of the piece depends on whether
the firing has been done properly.

Types of kilns

A kiln can de defined as an oven in which a series of physical and chemical transformations occur that are necessary to carry out the firing of a piece.

Many different types of kilns are available. When buying one, it is important to take into account where it will be installed, whether there is an adequate source of electricity or gas, and whether ceramics is going to be the main or secondary activity. One thing is certain, however, the kiln must be resistant enough to withstand the changes in temperature.

Electric kilns

The electric kiln is something that all potters should have for running tests. It is easy and inexpensive to use. It maintains the temperature for a long time, and there is little heat loss.

Also, it has the advantage of not requiring supervision during the firing process. It is usually equipped with a microprocessor that allows the firing specifications to be set in advance. It also has a contact switch located on the door as a safety measure; by simply opening it the power is disconnected.

The one drawback of this kiln is that firing can only be done with oxides.

Electric kiln insulated with refractory fiber.

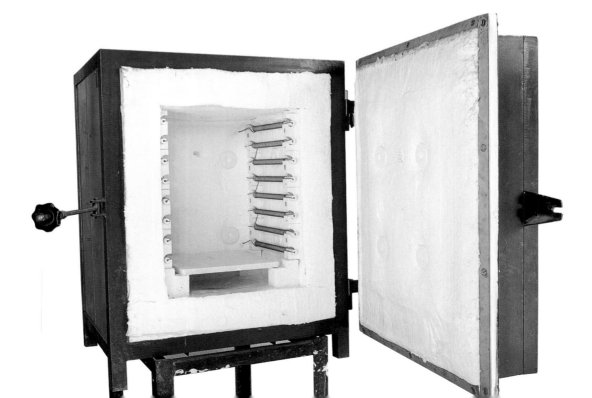

Gas kilns

The gas kiln is more appropriate for experienced potters, because it requires supervision during the entire firing session.

The advantage of using a gas kiln is that it allows control of the firing atmosphere, making it easy to promote a reducing atmosphere. The effects produced with a gas kiln and an oxidizing atmosphere are similar to the results achieved with an electric kiln.

Knowing how to operate the kiln is very important, because firing with propane tanks requires special attention to control the gas, the air, and its pressure. It is important to remember that safety rules require the installation of gas tanks outdoors and properly distanced from the kiln.

In terms of the baking time—and therefore the cost—gas kilns are twice as efficient as electric kilns. Also, gas kilns can reach the desired temperature more quickly than electric kilns.

A gas kiln is vital in areas where the electricity is expensive, so once you know how to operate this kiln, your results will be that much better.

Gas kilns equipped with four and six burners, respectively.

View of a jet on a gas kiln, equipped with a handle to control the pressure, and a safety valve.

Wood kilns

The wood kiln became almost obsolete when gas and electric kilns made their appearance and simplified the production process.

However, the wood kiln is necessary to achieve certain firing characteristics, which are usually spectacular and creative. Its use implies a total control of the firing process, which takes longer than with electric and gas kilns. The wood that fuels the kiln must be completely dry, and it is best if it is a hard burning wood.

Vase fired in a wood kiln, in a reduction atmosphere.

It is advisable to use hot burning firewood to feed the potter's kiln.

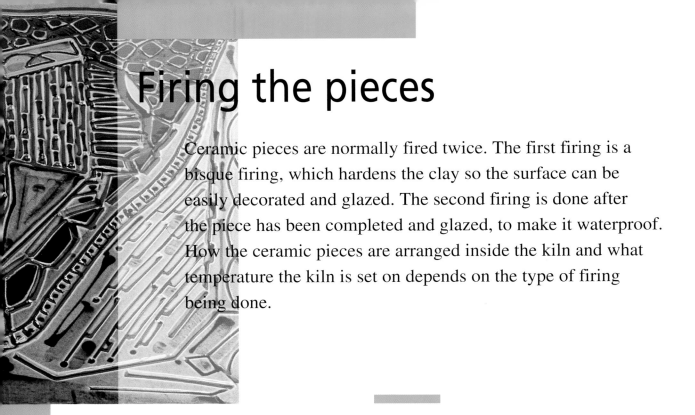

Firing the pieces

Ceramic pieces are normally fired twice. The first firing is a bisque firing, which hardens the clay so the surface can be easily decorated and glazed. The second firing is done after the piece has been completed and glazed, to make it waterproof. How the ceramic pieces are arranged inside the kiln and what temperature the kiln is set on depends on the type of firing being done.

Arranging the pieces in the kiln

Arranging the pieces inside the kiln re-quires calculated and strict planning, otherwise they could warp or even break. So it must be taken into consid-eration whether the pieces are being bisque fired or glaze fired.

Arranging the pieces for bisque firing

During the bisque-firing process, the clay—which has not yet been glazed—loses the water and acquires the porosi-ty needed for the surface to properly absorb the glaze that will be applied later. In this first firing, pieces can be placed one on top of the other, because they have not been glazed. However, keep in mind that if the kiln is too full, the firing time will be longer. Before the pieces are arranged in the kiln, they should be completely dry.

Pieces arranged in the kiln for bisque firing.

Arranging the pieces for glaze firing

For glaze firing, pieces must be arranged in such way that they do not come in contact with one another during the firing process, otherwise they can stick to each other when the glaze melts. Also, the kiln should not be too full, because the pieces will retain the heat longer than is necessary, or too empty, because the kiln will cool down too fast, and the glaze will be distributed unevenly.

Bats are used to arrange the glazed pieces in the kiln, and they can be purchased in specialized stores in different sizes and widths. Props can be purchased to support the bats. However, the bats must be coated with a mixture of 60 percent alumina and 40 percent kaolin before they are placed in the kiln, so that if any piece sticks to the bat, it is easy to clean. The life of the bats is also prolonged.

Supports, called star stilts, are also available to raise the pots, preventing them from adhering to the bat when the glaze melts. These supports are also sold in specialized stores. The star stilts are made of a refractory material—that is, of the same wire used to manufacture the electrical resistors of the kiln. However, they can only be used with temperatures of 1,868°F (1,020°C) and lower.

Notice how the glazed pieces should be placed in the kiln for firing. Star stilts prevent the objects from sticking to the bats.

Star stilts, made of a special wire.

It is advisable to coat the bats with a mixture of alumina and kaolin before the glazed pieces are fired.

Controlling the firing temperature

The temperature of the kiln is very important because it permanently changes the pieces being fired. Therefore, it is advisable to know exactly which changes are occurring at every moment.

Because the kiln door cannot be opened during the firing process, you will need to use another method for verifying the temperature and keeping it under control. One method involves using a pyrometer, which is a type of a thermometer that gives a direct reading of the temperature; the other involves using cones, which are made of a mixture of melting materials. These cones are also known as melting cones or Seger cones.

Cones

Cones are made of different clay materials, which, through a mathematical calculation, melt at a determined temperature, from 1,112°F to 2,732°F (600°C to 1,500°C). They come stamped with a reference number. It is advisable to have a reference table handy, to ensure that the correct cone is used in each firing. The cones should be placed inside, near the kiln's door, in front of the peephole.

It is important to pay attention to the melting of the cones during the first firings, to check the temperature marked by the pyrometer. For example, if a cone marked 1,832°F (1,000°C) is placed inside a kiln whose temperature is also programmed at 1,832°F (1,000°C) and that cone does not bend when the door of the kiln is opened, it means that the kiln is not baking at 1,832°F (1,000°C). Therefore, a second firing would need to be done, again placing a 1,832°F (1,000°C) cone inside, but this time the pyrometer should say 1,868°F (1,020°C). If upon opening the door the cone

Pyrometer

The pyrometer is an instrument for measuring the temperature of the kiln. It is made of a thermoelectric element, or thermopar, consisting of two wires that are welded at one end and covered with a porcelain tube. The welded tip is placed inside the kiln, and the loose ends are connected to a dial, which registers the temperature.

Nowadays, the quality of the pyrometers that come with small kilns is not very good, and they usually do not provide an accurate reading. The margin of error should be registered at the beginning using Seger cones. Once that has been established, the cones are no longer needed.

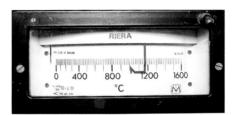

Pyrometers are available in both digital (above) and analog (below).

This picture illustrates where and how the cone must be placed before the firing begins.

bends, it means that the pyrometer has a difference of 68°F (20°C). Therefore, when you wish to fire at 1,832°F (1,000°C), the pyrometer should be set for 1,868°F (1,020°C).

Cones are often used because they are the most reliable tool available for measuring the firing temperature.

SEGER CONES							
Melting Point °F	Cone No.	Chemical Composition					
1,652	010a	—	—	—	—	—	—
1,688	09a	0.5 Na_2O	0.5 PbO	—	0.8 Al_2O_3	0.1 B_2O_3	3.6 SiO_2
1,724	08a	0.3 K_2O	0.7 CaO	0.2 Fe_2O_3	0.3 Al_2O_3	0.5 B_2O_3	3.5 SiO_2
1,760	07a	0.3 K_2O	0.7 CaO	0.2 Fe_2O_3	0.3 Al_2O_3	0.45 B_2O_3	3.55 SiO_2
1,796	06a	0.5 K_2O	0.7 CaO	0.2 Fe_2O_3	0.3 Al_2O_3	0.40 B_2O_3	3.60 SiO_2
1,832	05a	0.3 K_2O	0.7 CaO	0.2 Fe_2O_3	0.3 Al_2O_3	0.35 B_2O_3	3.65 SiO_2
1,868	04a	0.3 K_2O	0.7 CaO	0.2 Fe_2O_3	0.3 Al_2O_3	0.30 B_2O_3	3.70 SiO_2
1,904	03a	0.3 K_2O	0.7 CaO	0.2 Fe_2O_3	0.3 Al_2O_3	0.25 B_2O_3	3.75 SiO_2
1,940	02a	0.3 K_2O	0.7 CaO	0.2 Fe_2O_3	0.3 Al_2O_3	0.20 B_2O_3	3.80 SiO_2
1,976	01a	0.3 K_2O	0.7 CaO	0.2 Fe_2O_3	0.3 Al_2O_3	0.10 B_2O_3	3.85 SiO_2
2,012	1a	0.3 K_2O	0.7 CaO	0.2 Fe_2O_3	0.3 Al_2O_3	0.05 B_2O_3	3.90 SiO_2

Types of firing

Sometimes it is necessary to fire the modeled clay lightly so it acquires the hardness necessary for decorating it. This first process is called bisque firing, because the clay acquires the consistency of a biscuit—that is, the porosity required to properly absorb the glaze that will be applied later.

During the first phase of the firing, the temperature should be about 302°F (150°C), which is when the piece releases the water contained in the body. From this point on, it must increase slowly until it reaches 1,652°F or 1,760°F (900°C or 960°C), which is when the clay turns bisque.

Another type of firing is when the finished and glazed piece is baked to waterproof it. In this case the firing process is more complex and longer.

If the piece is baked only once, it is referred to as single fired; if it is baked twice, the first being bisque fired, it is referred to as glaze fired.

Baked pieces, with the glaze.

Firing curve

The firing of clay goes through different phases, where the appropriate time and temperatures are decisive factors for achieving optimum results. Therefore you must know and control the firing curve exactly.

This curve is divided into six times, which correspond to the warming phases, or increases in temperature. The cooling phase is less important, because it does not always follow the same pattern. However, you must pay attention at the moment when the temperature lowers from 1,112°F to 752°F (600°C to 400°C), and try to make this happen slowly. The cooling period can last a few hours or several days.

First firing phase

This first phase, from around 32°F to 392°F (0°C to 200°C) is the drying process, and lasts about two hours. During this time the piece releases water contained in the body. The door of the kiln must be kept ajar (¾ to 1¼ inches [2 to 3 cm] should be enough) during this period so the vapors created during the drying can escape. This will prevent moisture from forming on the walls, avoiding oxidation of the metal.

Second firing phase

During the second phase, from around to 392°F to 752°F (200°C to 400°C), all water that was chemically combined and that is contained in the piece is released. If the firing occurs too fast, the pieces can explode either because there is excess moisture inside of them or because there is an air bubble. This is a very delicate phase of the firing process and lasts about two hours.

Before the pieces are placed inside the kiln, you must make sure they are completely dry. Otherwise, they may be ruined during the second phase of the firing, like the bowl in the picture.

Third firing phase

The third phase, from around 752°F to 1,112°F (400°C to 600°C), is known as the quartz transformation. During this process a sudden change occurs in the quartz, causing its volume to increase. Therefore, the pieces go through a transformation, and if the temperature increases too fast, they could break in half. The approximate duration of this phase is two hours.

This phenomenon happens twice during the firing—when the kiln heats up and when it cools down. It is advisable to let the kiln cool down slowly during this interval.

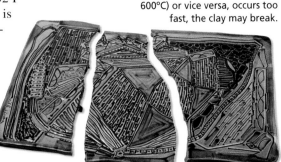

If the change of temperature from 752°F to 1,112°F (400°C to 600°C) or vice versa, occurs too fast, the clay may break.

Fourth firing phase

During the fourth phase, from around 1,112°F to 1,472°F (600°C to 800°C), nothing special happens inside the kiln, which is why the piece is referred to as free time. The temperature can be accelerated depending on need, and between ten minutes and one hour should be devoted to this phase of the firing.

Fifth firing phase

During the fifth phase, from around 1,472°F to 1,832°F (800°C to 1,000°C), one must think about the type of firing that is being done. If it is a bisque firing, the temperature can be increased to 1,760°F or 1,796°F (960°C or 980°C) in the space of one to one and a half hours, depending on whether or not the kiln is full.

If the pieces are glazed, a longer time should be reserved so the kiln can heat up evenly and the different coats of the glaze, whose boiling point begins at 1,472°F (800°C), can be fired correctly. In two and a half to three hours, the temperature must go from around 1,472°F to 1,832°F (800°C to 1,000°C). This is called the glaze maturation phase.

Sixth firing phase

The sixth and last phase of the firing corresponds to the maintenance time. This step is not always necessary, and it is usually done for kilns that bake too fast or in firing processes where the kiln generates even-out temperatures. The time is also optional, and you can decide on that as you become more acquainted with the kiln. Time may vary from thirty minutes to one hour.

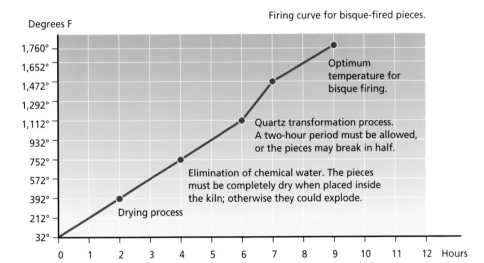

Firing curve for bisque-fired pieces.

Degrees F

Optimum temperature for bisque firing.

Quartz transformation process. A two-hour period must be allowed, or the pieces may break in half.

Elimination of chemical water. The pieces must be completely dry when placed inside the kiln; otherwise they could explode.

Drying process

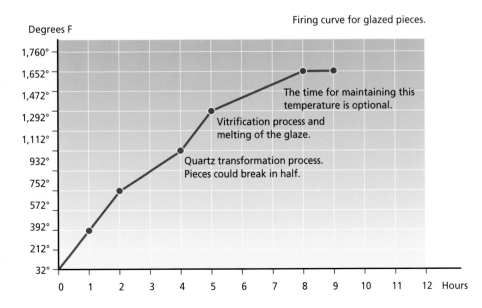

Firing curve for glazed pieces.

Degrees F

The time for maintaining this temperature is optional.

Vitrification process and melting of the glaze.

Quartz transformation process. Pieces could break in half.

Emptying the kiln

Care must be taken when opening the door of the kiln. Be aware that if the door is opened too fast when the temperature is still high, it could cause the pieces or the bats to break. Therefore it is advisable to wait until the kiln cools off. The ideal temperature for emptying the kiln without any risk varies between 212°F and 248°F (100°C and 120°C). However, even when the kiln is sufficiently cool, the pieces may still be quite hot, which is why it is recommended to leave the kiln open for about 30 minutes before taking the pieces out.

Pieces baked with glaze, just taken out of the kiln. Work by Dolors Ros.

Atmosphere

The atmosphere of the kiln is an important factor to consider when choosing which kiln to purchase.

Kilns either have an oxidizing or a reducing atmosphere. Electric kilns can only generate an oxidizing atmosphere. Gas and wood kilns, on the other hand, can create both types of atmospheres.

Oxidizing atmosphere

It is said that a kiln has an oxidizing atmosphere when there is too much oxygen inside of it. Despite this excess, such an atmosphere does not change the materials the pottery piece is made of.

Bisque firing occurs in an oxidizing atmosphere, during which time the clay releases its water, achieving the appropriate porosity.

Reduction atmosphere

It is said that a reduction of atmosphere exists when combustion takes place—that is, when the carbons combine with the air's oxygen to form carbon dioxide. If there is an inadequate amount of oxygen in the combustion, a release of carbon and carbon dioxide occurs, causing smoke to form. If this process takes place in a closed kiln, the carbon dioxide that is released will attempt to obtain oxygen from the closest source, and that will be the pieces that are inside the kiln. Therefore, the basic materials used in these pieces will react chemically. This change originating from the loss of oxygen is known as reduction, and because of its effects, the colors of the affected materials are altered.

It is easy to create this kind of atmosphere in any type of combustion kiln. The most spectacular results are achieved with copper oxides, which turn green in an oxidizing atmosphere and red in a reduction atmosphere. Iron oxides turn yellow in an oxidizing atmosphere and green in a reduction atmosphere.

Vase fired in a reduction atmosphere with copper oxide. Work by Marta Rocabado.

Bowl produced in an oxidizing atmosphere, with copper oxide and alkaline frit.

Piece fired in a reduction atmosphere with iron oxide.

Solving or avoiding problems and mistakes

Most mistakes made during the production of a pottery piece are due to the lack of knowledge of the characteristics of the raw materials being used.

The defects that appear during the decoration process are easy to fix, because there is still time to correct or to modify the piece. If the error occurs during firing, however, then the defects may be permanent.

Pieces with engobe

• How to avoid fingerprints in a piece recently coated with engobe

The piece should be coated in two stages and should not be touched when it is wet.

To prevent fingerprints on pieces coated with engobe, one side is covered first, and left until the engobe becomes leather hard. Then you should be able to hold it with the fingers without leaving fingerprints.

• How to prevent an engobe from flaking off after baking

The engobe should not be applied when the object is too dry.

Neither the engobe nor the glaze coat should be too thick.

The kiln should not cool down too fast, otherwise contraction will occur too suddenly.

The engobe has flaked off of this piece.

It is important for the engobe to be of the proper density.

• Avoiding lumps when the engobe is applied

Lumps may appear if the engobe has not been sifted with an 80-screen sieve.

• Preventing a piece that has been coated with engobe from looking as if it did not have engobe after the glazing

The engobe should always be of the proper density, and the object should not be subjected to a temperature that is too high.

Before using liquid engobe, sift it with an 80-screen sieve.

In decoration

• When the decoration created with engobe comes off before the firing
It may mean that the color was too thick. In this case, the only solution is to add water.

It may also be that the plasticity between the two clays is not the appropriate one. Then 5 percent quartz should be added to the color.

• When the decorations applied with oxides diluted with water smear all over the surface
Oxide by itself always tends to smear, especially if a lead frit is used. Therefore, the oxide must be mixed with a fixative, such as engobe or any white clay, in approximate proportions of 10 percent to 20 percent.

When engobe is applied over dry clay, the type of cracking shown in the picture may occur.

If the piece is going to be glazed with a lead frit, the dye must be mixed with a pinch of engobe or frit so it does not come off.

• When the decorations that are applied using dyes diluted with water come out of the kiln separated from the glaze
This problem may occur if the dye is too thick. Therefore, it should always be applied very watery. As an added measure, it is advisable to add a fixative, such as 20 percent engobe, or 20 percent low temperature frit.

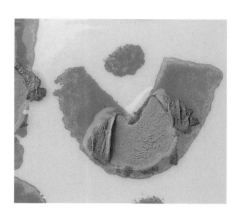

In firing

• Bubbles in the pieces after firing
If the layer of glaze is too thick, if the kiln has not reached the proper temperature, or if the pieces were fired too quickly during the last phase, the pieces may develop bubbles.

Bubbles can result from very fast firing or the lack of firing.

• Pieces broken in half
If the pieces were fired too quickly during the phase (known as transformation of the quartz), or if the oven cooled down too quickly in the firing process, from 1,112°F to 752°F (600°C to 400°C), you may find that the pieces break in half.

Refer to the temperature curves of the previous chapter.

• Pieces adhered to the bats after firing
This may mean that star stilts were not used. It may also mean that too much glaze was applied to the objects or that the firing temperature was too high.

• The cone has not bent
It may mean that the wrong cone was chosen, or that the indicator on the kiln's pyrometer was not calibrated.

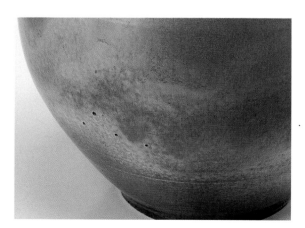

Seger cone before being used.

The same cone after being fired.

Glossary

A
Alumina
Substance that controls the viscosity of the glaze and adheres it to the surface.
Appliqué
A relief made with a mold for decorating objects.

B
Ball mill
A machine that consists of a rotating container full of flint pebbles that is used to grind the frit after it comes out of the kiln.
Bisque, or biscuit
Unglazed pottery baked at a low temperature.
Bisque firing
The preliminary firing of the raw clay.

C
Channels
Grooves made in certain pieces for decorative purposes.
Cones
Pyramid-shaped objects made of clay and melting materials that bend at specific temperatures. They are used to measure the real temperature of the kiln.
Contraction
The shrinkage that the clay suffers from the evaporation of the water contained in it.
Crackle
Decorative cracks created on the glazed surface during firing, caused by the different rates of dilation and contraction of the glaze and the clay.
Crawling
When the engobe or the glaze separates from the body after firing.
Crazing
Involuntary crackling of the glaze.

D
Density gauge
Instrument used to measure the density of the engobes and the glazes.
Double boiler
Method for heating something placed in a container, which is itself inserted into another filled with water, and placed on the stove so the contents heat up gradually and consistently.

E
Earthenware
White clay, generally calciferous and very porous.
Elasticity
Quality of the clay that allows it to be worked without breaking.
Engobe
White or red clay that is used to cover another clay or to correct its defects. It can also be used for decorative purposes.

F
Firing curve
Line of a graphic that reflects the relationship between the increase or the decrease of the temperature and the baking time.
Flux
Low-melting substance that reduces the melting point of other materials.
Frit
A glaze mixture made up of ingredients that have been previously fired.
Frit (low fire)
Very low firing frit that is used to mix with the dyes to prevent them from separating from the glaze.

G
Glaze firing
This refers to the second firing, which pottery pieces are subjected to in order to make them waterproof. It follows the bisque firing.

Grog
Clay that is bisque fired and ground into various sized particles. This material, which is not plastic, aides the drying of the pastes, and increases the resistance of the objects during baking.

Gypsum
Mixture of plaster of paris and water. It is used for casting.

Inlay
The area of an object filled with colored clay.

Kaolin
White natural clay that bakes at high temperatures.

Latex
Material that is used for resist decoration.

Leather hard
The condition of semihardness of the clay, when it still has part of the moisture.

Majolica
Low-fire white clay, covered with a tin lead glaze.

Pigment
Raw materials that are mixed with other substances in the form of oxides and dyes and used as coloring agents.

Plaster of paris
Hydrate of calcium sulfate, which is baked and ground. It hardens very rapidly if mixed with water and kneaded. It is used to make molds.

Plasticity
The quality of clay that allows it to be molded.

Porcelain
Ceramic paste made from kaolin, feldspar, and quartz. It becomes white after being fired at high temperatures.

Potash soap
Soap that is applied to the surface of the mold to prevent it from sticking to the clay.

Pressing
The exercise of applying pressure on the clay to make a decoration in a mold.

Pyrometer
An instrument for measuring the temperature of the kiln during baking.

Quartz
Crystallized silica found in nature with multiple forms and properties, depending on its size and purity.

Refractory
Material that is resistant to fire or to very high temperatures.

Scratching
Indentation made with a tool on leather hardware, for the purpose of decorating it.

Serrated scraper
A piece of saw blade sharpened by the user.

Sgraffito
Decorating technique used when the clay is leather hard. It consists of scratching a layer of engobe to show the surface underneath.

Silica
The most abundant chemical element on Earth. It forms part of numerous minerals and rocks, among them clay.

Single fire
The term applied to clays that have been baked only once.

Slip
Thick liquid suspension made of one or more types of clay mixed with water. It is normally used to bond two pieces together.

Star stilt
A tripod-like device used to support the glazed pieces inside the kiln.

Trailer (slip)
Tool used for decorating with engobes, especially for making lines and dots.

Turntable
A platform that turns on an axis, on top of which the piece to be worked is placed.

Vitrification
The moment when the glaze begins to melt in the kiln.

Wheel
Horizontal disc that turns on a vertical axis and is propelled by a pedal or a motor.

ACKNOWLEDGMENTS

To Pilar Basomba for referring my name to María Fernanda.

To Marc Ribas, my son, for his constant support and encouragement.

To Yukiko Murata, who has collaborated and worked so hard in the production of the pieces.

To Olga Piqué, who was a key person at the beginning in helping me get started.

To María Fernanda Canal, for her great professionalism and discipline in the entire working process, and for her help in organizing each of the chapters properly.

To Eva Bargalló, Tomàs Ubach, and the entire team from Parramón Ediciones, S.A., for their help and advice in the editing process.

To Joan Soto, who in addition to being a great photographer, and having great patience, has become a great friend. His advice, with his knowledge of publishing, has avoided much unnecessary work.

To my best friends, who have taken the time to encourage me and to endure my bad moods during the difficult times of the project.

To the *Escola de Ceràmica* of Biscal, a teaching center that was founded by me in 1972, and where this book was written. I want to thank all the people there who oversee the administrative duties for their collaboration during the entire production process.

To *Bisbal, Materials for Pottery,* who have put at my disposal all the materials needed for photography.

To *Cerámicas Vila-Clara,* where they opened the doors for me for all types of work.

To *Cerámicas Pordamsa,* who have allowed me to do all the sessions that were needed.

CERAMICS

© Copyright for the English edition for the United States, Canada, its territories and possessions by Barron's Educational Series, Inc. 2002

Original title of the book in Spanish: *Cerámica*

© Copyright 2001 by Parramon Ediciones, S.A. — World Rights
Published in 2001 by Parramon Ediciones, S.A., Barcelona, Spain

Translated from the Spanish by Michael Brunelle and Beatríz Cortabarria

All rights reserved.
No part of this book may be reproduced in any form, by photostat, microfilm, xerography, or any other means, or incorporated into any informational retreival system, electronic or mechanical, without the written permission of the copyright owner.

All inquiries should be addressed to:
Barron's Educational Series, Inc.
250 Wireless Blvd.
Hauppauge, NY 11788
www.barronseduc.com

International Standard Book No. 0-7641-2163-4

*Library of Congress Catalog Card
No. 2002103819*

Editor :
Mª. Fernanda Canal

Projects:
Dolors Ros and Yukiko Murata

Photography:
Estudio Nos & Soto

Drawings:
Jaume Farrés

Printed in Spain
9 8 7 6 5 4 3 2 1